GARY RICHMOND

Forward by Charles Swindoll
Photography by Gary Richmond

DMJ Media Group • La Mirada, California
www.dmjmedia.com

LCCN: 2005921217

ISBN 0-9765829-0-2

Printed in the United States of America

First Edition, March 2005

Portions of this book were originally published in *A View from the Zoo* (1987), *Please Don't Feed The Bears* (1990), and *Life Is a Zoo* (1992). Copyrights of all original publications owned by Gary Richmond.

To Hayley, Kendall, Colby, Katie and Aiden

It is a far more wonderful privilege than I had
every imagined…being your grandfather.
Every smile, loving look, little hug, wave goodbye,
and kiss on the cheek makes me so happy and
so thankful thta God gave you to me.
I wanted you to grow up knowing that
Papa and Grandma love you so much
that we dedicated this book to you.

TABLE OF CONTENTS

FOREWARD

Gary Richmond and I have known each other for years. I was drawn to him before he became a member of our pastoral team at the First Evangelical Free Church of Fullerton, California.

He is an absolute joy to be around: genuine charisma, quick wit, a zest for life, and always a story or two to add flavor to the moment. His years at the Los Angeles Zoo have given him an enormous depth of appreciation for the animal world. His even greater number of years in vocational Christian service have given him a breadth of understanding of people like you and me. In my opinion, his ability to use the former to illustrate the latter is unparalleled. I know of no one better qualified to communicate truth for today from this unique perspective than Gary.

In additional to being a splendid storyteller and one with a keen awareness of human nature, the man is a fine husband, a devoted father, and a dear friend. I am pleased he accepted the challenge to put his wealth of unusual experiences into print. More than merely "a view from the zoo," these pages contain one mirror after another reflecting images of and insights into ourselves. I suggest, therefore, that you not hurry through these pages. Walk slowly. Pause thoughtfully. There is much to be gleaned from these creatures God has made through the pen of a man God has gifted.

Chuck Swindoll
Pastor, Radio Teacher, Author

This Foreward originally appeared in *A View From the Zoo* published in 1987.

THANK YOU...

In the better part of a lifetime there are just a handful of people that leave their fingerprint on your soul. I thank God for these people...

Carol, my wife, the mother of our children, the world's best grandmother and my closest friend, you're the best.

Dr. Charles Sedgwick DVM, my close friend, whose scholarship, ability to teach, love for wild aniimals and kindness to people have been a wonderful inspiration for many years now.

To George Burch, the primary Bible teacher in my life. George is a Godly man and I rarely teach without teaching something George taught me.

To longtime friends who matter a great deal to me (listed in no particular order): Jim, Sonny, Dale, Mark, Scott, Keith, Mike, Paul, Steve, John, Dave, Jay, Connie, and Linda.

To my Father, Walter Richmond. You're still my hero. See you in not so very long.

But ask the beasts, and they will teach you;
the birds of the air, and they will tell you;
or the plants of the earth, and they will teach you;
and the fish of the sea will declare to you.
Who among all these does not know
that the hand of the LORD has done this?

Job 12:7–9

I began my career with the zoo in 1967. It was a golden time. It will never be like that in the zoo world again. It's because the earth is smaller now and the numbers of animals have declined.

The Los Angeles Zoo was the only zoo in history to begin as a major zoo. We saw rare and endangered animals being brought to us in a steady, magnificent stream. The experience was a hands-on gathering unprecedented since the time of Noah—a great adventure.

It is with great joy that I share some of my best stories with you in hopes of honoring the One who allowed me my golden time, the One who fashioned the animals about which I have written. Come and join me now in my larger-than-life experience. And laugh a little. This isn't just my view from the zoo…it's for all of us. As you turn the pages you will see that life itself is a zoo!

Gary Richmond

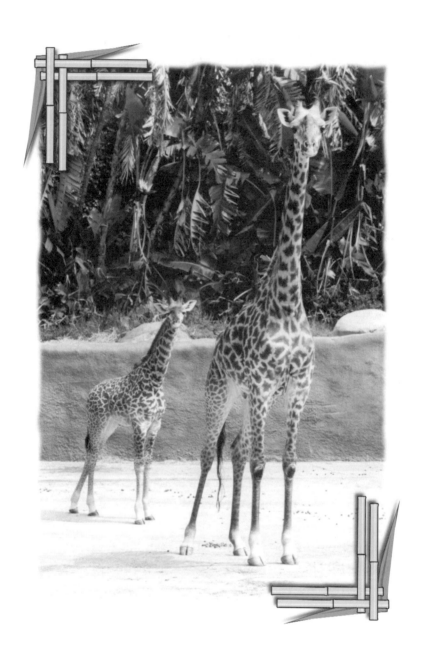

Ups and Downs

God has designed thousands of ways for the animal kingdom to come into existence, but in my estimation the birth of the baby giraffe is of all births the most impressive. See it once and you'll never forget it.

The zoo health center was called at 9:30 a.m. and we were informed that the female Angola giraffe was giving birth. If the veterinarian and I wanted to watch we could. Neither of us had ever witnessed a giraffe birth before, so we headed quickly for the giraffe barn. We parked and walked quietly to a location where about seven of us were afforded an earthbound view of an elevated event. I sat on a bale of hay next to Jack Badal, a man considered by most of us to be the greatest animal keeper alive. He was a man of few and well-chosen words, and when I sat down, he only nodded and continued to suck the sweetness from the alfalfa stem he had pulled from the hay bale on which we sat.

I noticed the calf's front hooves and head were already visible and dripping with amniotic fluids. I also noticed that the mother was standing up. "When is she going to lie down?" I said to Jack, who still hadn't said anything.

"She won't," he answered.

"But her hindquarters are nearly ten feet off the ground. That

7

calf might get hurt from the fall," I said. Jack just gave me that look that told me I had probably said something that revealed my ignorance.

I wondered why no plans were being made to procure a fireman's net to catch the baby, so I asked. "Listen, Gary," he said. "You can go try to catch the calf if you want, but remember that its mother has enough strength in her hind legs to kick your head off, which is what she'd do if you get anywhere near that calf. They've killed lions that tried to get their calves."

I was able to sit quietly for a while and observe the calf's journey down the birth canal. Its neck and front legs were fully extended and dangling freely, ten feet above the hard ground on which it was soon to fall. It seemed unbelievable to me that in just a few minutes this newborn was going to be introduced to such trauma. Ten feet! To the hard ground! (It had taken me twelve years to get up the nerve to jump off a high dive approximately ten feet high into clear deep water. This giraffe calf was going to top that during its first thirty minutes of visible existence.)

The moment we had anticipated was not a disappointment. The calf, a plucky male, hurled forth, falling ten feet and landing on his back. Within seconds, he rolled to an upright position with his legs tucked under his body. From this position he considered the world for the first time, shaking some of the last vestiges of birthing fluids from his eyes and ears.

The mother giraffe lowered her head long enough to take a quick look. Then she positioned herself so that she was standing directly over the calf. She waited for about a minute and then did the most unreasonable thing. She swung her pendulous leg outward and kicked her baby, so that is was sent sprawling head over heels (or hooves, in this case). I turned to Jack and exclaimed, "Why'd she do that?"

"She wants it to get up, and if it doesn't she'll do it again."

Jack was right—the violent process was repeated again and then again. The struggle to rise was momentous, and as the baby grew tired of trying, the mother would again stimulate its efforts with a hearty kick.

Finally, amidst the cheers of the animal care staff, the calf stood for the first time. Wobbly, for sure, but it stood. Then we were struck silent when she kicked it off its feet again.

Jack's face was the only face not expressing astonishment. "She wants it to remember how it got up," he offered. "That's why she knocked it down. In the wild it would need to get up as soon as possible to follow the herd. The mother needs the herd, too. Lions, hyenas, leopards, and hunting dogs all would enjoy young giraffes. They'd get it, too, if the mother didn't teach her baby to quickly get up and get with it."

Jack waved good-bye with his alfalfa stem and returned to his section to care for his animals, something he did better than anyone I have ever known.

I've thought about the birth of that giraffe many times since that spring morning and have seen its parallel in my own life. There have been many times when it seemed that I had just stood after a trial only to be knocked down by the next. It was God helping me to remember how it was that I got up, urging me always to walk with Him in His shadow under His care.

> Count it all joy, my brethren, when you meet various trials, for you know that the testing of your faith produces steadfastness.
>
> James 1:2–3

Be Careful! You Might Let Out a Bear

I'll never forget the feelings I experienced when two shiny new keys were pressed firmly into my trembling hands. They weren't just any keys. These keys gave me access to all the cages at the Los Angeles Zoo. The supervisor, a crusty veteran, admonished me solemnly concerning the use and care of these keys.

"Richmond," he said, "these keys will let you in to care for millions of dollars worth of animals. Some of them could never be replaced, but you could be, if you catch my drift. Some of the animals would hurt themselves if they got out, and more significantly, they might hurt and even kill somebody. You wouldn't want that on your conscience.

"And, Richmond, don't lose the keys. The big boys in administration don't take it too well if you lose the keys. It works out best if they don't hear your name much until you pass probation six months from now."

The longer we talked the heavier the keys became. I discovered that most of the veterans (five years or more of service) had let out animals. And if I stayed at the zoo, sooner or later it would happen to me. Somehow my job security was tied to how I cared for these keys, and they seemed heavier still.

He gave me several tips on key care, use and safety, and

emphasized the value of getting into a routine. "Consistency is your best safeguard," he said. "Do it the same way at every exhibit. Develop a good habit and don't vary your routine."

I took him seriously and performed flawlessly for four months. I received sterling evaluations for my safety habits—then something happened.

I couldn't tell you why my routine varied, but somehow it did and with the most dangerous animal at the zoo. Ivan was a polar bear who weighed well over nine hundred pounds and had killed two prospective mates. He hated people and never missed an opportunity to attempt to grab anyone passing by his cage. Many of us had experienced nightmares featuring Ivan. And one of the thoughts most discussed among the keepers was the horrifying question, "What if Ivan got out?"

For more than one hundred consecutive workdays I had cared for this nightmare, never coming close to making a mistake. Then I let him out of his night quarters into the sparkling morning sunshine by pulling a lever which lifted a five-hundred pound steel guillotine door. No sooner had he passed under it than I realized that I had left the steel door that had given me access to the outside exhibit (where he now was) wide open. At any minute he might be walking down the hall and around the corner. My inclination was to run. Not wanting to be fired, I chose to stay. I lifted the guillotine door again, and to my relief Ivan was in view. He was a creature of routine, and he always spent the first hour of his morning pacing. His pattern was L-shaped. He would walk from the door five steps straight out and then turn right for three steps. He would then rock back and forth and come back to the guillotine door, which he would bump with his head. He would repeat that cycle for one hour and then rest.

I timed his pacing cycle and determined that I had seventeen seconds to run down the hallway and shut the open door. I staked my life on his consistency. He didn't seem to notice the wide-open door, which was unusual. Animals tend to notice any changes in their environment.

I decided that when he made his next turn, I would run down the L-shaped concrete hallway hoping upon hope that I would not see Ivan.

He turned and I ran. With every step my knees weakened. My heart pounded so hard I felt sure it would burst from fear. I made the corner and faced the critical moment. Ivan was still out of sight; I lunged for the door handle. As I reached out for the handle, I looked to the right. There was the bear, eight feet away. Our eyes met. His were cold and unfeeling and I'm sure mine expressed all the terror that filled the moment. The door clanged shut and the clasp was secured. My knees buckled and I fell to the floor racked with the effects of too much adrenaline. I looked up and Ivan was staring at me through the viewing window of the hallway door.

I had almost let out a bear—the worst bear at the zoo.

Recently, our church family studied disciplines that could help us stand firm in our faith. The development of good habits is one of the keys to our becoming mature. Consider Hebrews 5:14:

> But solid food is for the mature, who because of practice have their senses trained to discern good and evil.

Consistent living produces its own protection. Seek it. Cherish it. Desire it. It may keep you from letting out a bear.

BACK-UP MAN

I always felt good about going into a cage with Bob Pedersen. He was the best back-up man in the business. I was sure that if something went wrong during a dangerous animal capture Bob would be there to do whatever was needed to bail me out. He felt comfortable with my abilities, and we really enjoyed working together.

When it is necessary to go into a cage and capture a potentially dangerous animal, the first rule of thumb is that there must always be two or more people to handle the animal effectively. The first man works the animal into position while the back-up man cuts off its avenues of escape. The roles can change back and forth when the animal changes position, but we usually decide who will catch and who will grab before we unlock the cage door.

Bob had excellent reaction time and he was strong. We netted and held everything from baboons to cheetahs, and neither of us ever sustained an injury when working together. In fact, the only time that I sustained any injuries was when I broke the cardinal rules of capture: 1) Never go into a cage alone, and 2) Never work with an inexperienced back-up.

It was a lazy summer afternoon in August and I had finished all that I had been assigned around the health center. I needed to get down to the North American section to vaccinate the arctic foxes for distemper, hepatitis, and leptospirosis. They were overdue. I picked up the phone to call the section, then set it down again as a young and beautiful Ph.D. candidate from the local university walked into the health center office. She glanced around, then asked me if there was anybody who could help her. I told her that I would if I could. She explained that she was doing a behavioral study on white-handed gibbon apes and needed to mark them with white paint so that she could readily tell which ape was which.

We drove down to the Eurasian section and I looked for the keeper who cared for the gibbons. He had already gone home for the day and I couldn't find anyone else who worked in the section. I noticed that the beautiful young scientist kept checking her watch.

"Running late?" I queried.

"Yes, and I was so hoping that we would be able to get the marking done today," she replied. She sounded so desperate, like maybe she wouldn't get her Ph.D. or maybe she would get an "F" on her assignment or something like that.

"It's just that I can't find anybody to do back-up and I'm not supposed to go into a capture situation alone," I explained.

"Gee, I'm really sorry to be putting you to so much trouble. Your gibbons must be more aggressive than the ones at the primate center. Ours were easy. I even helped. Hey, I would be glad to help you. I'll be your back-up."

"I'm sorry, I can't let you help. If you got bit, I'd get fired," I explained.

She sat there looking so disappointed, so dejected. I had to prove that chivalry was not dead, so I made a stupid decision.

"I guess it wouldn't hurt anything to try," I announced.

"Oh, thank you, thank you, thank you. You're a dear."

Perhaps "dunce" would have been a more appropriate word, but just for a minute there I felt like a dear. And it felt pretty good. I gathered the capture equipment together and carried it to the back of the gibbon cage. All three of the gibbons looked at the two hoop nets I was carrying and hooted their displeasure. Hand-over-hand they quickly retreated to the far end of the cage and huddled together for mutual comfort. They looked fairly intimidated, and I took that to be a good sign.

I entered the cage with confidence. I had learned to act confident whether I felt confident or not. It gave you a slight edge if the animals were on the defensive. I left one of the two nets leaning against the cage wall and began to make my advance. The apes headed in different directions and it looked like it would be every gibbon for itself. I made a beautiful pass of the net, and whoosh! I had a gibbon. I knew that it must have looked impressive and I twisted the net to make sure that the gibbon didn't accomplish a premature exit.

It was about that time that the other two attacked me with a vengeance. I couldn't have engendered more wrath if I had tried. That two remaining gibbons seemed to be coming at me from every direction at the same time. One got a large handful of my hair and decided to keep it. The other gibbon grabbed my arm with such force that he caused an impressive bruise. I wore it for more than a week. There is no dignified way to exit a cage while being swarmed by gibbons. I just did the best I could to get out without being bitten to pieces. That was exactly what the Flying Gibbonski Brothers had in mind. As I fell backward into the holding cage, the beautiful young scientist had the presence of mind to push the sliding door shut. The gibbons continued to reach through the chain link, hoping to pull me back out where they could work me over good. But I had backed just out of their reach.

Now there is really nothing clever that one can say when one has just proven himself to be a jerk, but one usually tries to say something. I know I did.

"Well, Miss, do you think this might be why they recommend that we never go into a cage by ourselves?"

"Maybe so," she answered with a smile that convinced me that I had looked as ridiculous as I felt.

I would have been grateful if we just could have left and forgotten that the whole thing had happened, but there was still the little matter of the one gibbon that I had netted. It was still neatly twisted and bagged and lying quietly on the cool cement floor. "Be sure your sins will find you out," I thought. I had no choice. I had to get someone to help me release the gibbon and retrieve the nets. I managed to get my supervisor to come back with me, and together we quickly accomplished what I had failed to do alone.

"Next time you break the rules to impress somebody you may lose a finger, an eye, or your life. Don't do that anymore, Richmond," he said sternly. We drove back to the health center silently, and I pondered my irresponsible actions. I never made that same mistake again. But I did make others.

We had just hired Dr. Reed, a brand new veterinarian who had just graduated from vet school. Dr. Reed had never worked with wild animals, and capture was something she had seen on television but had never participated in herself. She was nevertheless my supervisor, and I felt obligated to indulge her requests. She wanted to get some practice at capture, so she asked if I would please step aside and let her grab an adolescent greater kudu. A kudu is one of the largest antelopes, and though this young male only weighed a little over a hundred pounds he could still accomplish some serious damage with his formidable hooves. Dr. Reed would make the initial grab and control the head, the neck, and the front legs. She must keep it from falling to the ground or it would be in a great position to kick somebody's head off. I was the back-up, and my job was to control the hindquarters and keep it on its hind feet. The hindquarters are the business end, the end that can deliver the most damage.

Dr. Reed rushed in and exhibited a good deal of pluck as she grabbed the young kudu, I grabbed the hindquarters and our veterinary intern began to inject a large dose of penicillin. It was then that Dr. Reed lost her grip, and in trying to regain it she actually tipped the animal upside down. The kudu kicked upward with all of its might and knocked me temporarily unconscious. The hoof had passed through my open mouth and connected with the rear teeth on the opposite side of my head. My gums were bleeding profusely and all I could hear was a loud ringing in my ear. When things began to make sense again Dr. Reed was saying, "Tell me where you are. Tell me your name." After I had convinced her that I had fully returned to coherency, I was removed for medical treatment.

I made a decision that I would never again work without an experienced back-up or lead. I stuck to that decision for the last two years of my zoo career, and to my memory, I was never injured in a capture situation again.

So much of life lived at its best is a matter of surrounding ourselves with people who will provide good back-up. They will pull us out of trouble when we get into a mess. They will remind us that we are out of line and need to be playing by the rules. They will pour courage into us so that we can perform to the limits of our potential.

Because we reap what we sow it is necessary that we learn to be good back-up ourselves. The following is a list of responsibilities that go with being a good back-up person. If you have learned to love yourself and put yourself first, then you need not apply for this position, because it requires willingness to sacrifice and courage enough to live for others. The Christian version of back-up is called "one-anothering." As you read the following list, think of people in your life who are good at watching out for and caring for others.

John 15:12	Love one another.
Romans 5:13	Don't pass judgment on one another.
Romans 12:5	Be members of one another.
Romans 12:10	Be devoted to one another.
Romans 12:10	Honor one another.
Romans 12:16	Live in harmony with one another.
Romans 14:19	Build up one another.
Romans 15:5	Be like-minded toward one another
Romans 15:7	Accept one another.
I Corinthians 6:6	Don't make lawsuits again one another.
I Corinthians 12:25	Care for one another.
Galatians 5:13	Serve one another in love.
Galatians 5:15	Don't spitefully hurt one another.
Galatians 5:26	Don't provoke or envy one another.
Ephesians 4:32	Be kind to one another.
Ephesians 4:32	Forgive one another.
Ephesians 5:21	Submit to one another.
Colossians 3:9	Don't lie to one another.
Colossians 3:13	Teach and counsel one another.
I Thessalonians 3:12	Abound in love toward one another.

I Thessalonians 4:18	Comfort one another.
Titus 3:3	Don't hate one another.
Hebrews 3:13	Encourage one another.
Hebrews 10:24	Stir up one another to love and good deeds.
James 4:11	Don't slander one another.
James 5:9	Don't bear grudges against one another.
James 5:16	Confess your sins to one another.
James 5:16	Pray for one another.
I Peter 4:9	Offer hospitality to one another
I Peter 5:14	Greet one another.
I John 1:7	Have fellowship with one another.

Now that you've read the responsibilities of the ideal back-up person, try to think of the people in your life who fill that responsibility for you. Why don't you write or call them and thank them? They deserve it.

As you read through the list, did you see any verse that best stated some area of strength that you possess and use to support others? Was there a weak area?

Close the book and thank God for the back-up people in your life and your area of strength, and ask Him to help you grow in some specific area where you now show a weakness.

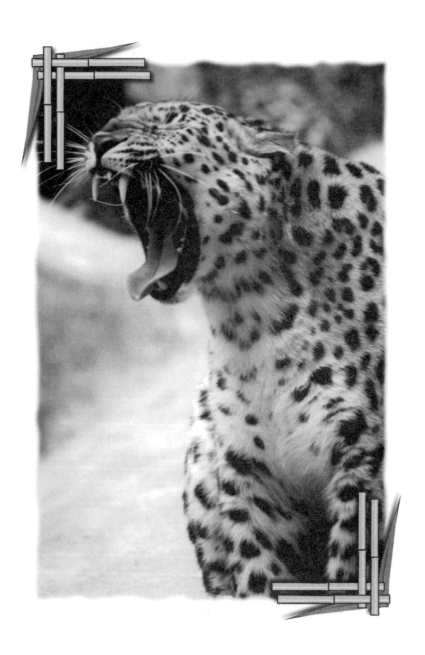

Nowhere To Go

If you think a South American jaguar is impressive when she bares her teeth and snarls from the confines of her cage, you should see her just after she's escaped. It's an experience that will continue to haunt you for weeks to come.

I was sitting at my desk updating the lowland gorilla's polio immunization records one afternoon when one of the guards from the zoo security force called.

"We've got ourselves an emergency," blurted the head of the security force. "A big cat got out of her cage and attacked a keeper. We need you and your boss right now!"

I ran for the lab where Dr. Bernstein was checking test results with our lab technician.

"We've got a hot one, Doc. Big cat's loose in the South America section. Probably a jaguar. Keeper's been hurt."

He nodded and we grabbed our emergency gear and headed for the truck. You know that these things will happen occasionally, but you never feel quite prepared when they do. We made speculation on who might have been hurt and hoped it was not too serious. A senior keeper ran to meet us as soon as the truck screeched to a halt in back of the jaguar exhibit. He filled us in while we got our equipment together. "Jaguar's loose, Doc. We'll need her tranquilized. She jumped Whittle. Looks like he'll be okay but his arm's broken. When the jag jumped him, he got his arm in her mouth. Security is taking him to the hospital now."

"Where's the public?" I inquired. I was 4:15 on a Monday afternoon. There wouldn't be a crowd, but there would be a few people wandering around.

"Yeah, we thought of that, too. We rounded them up and locked them in the restrooms till we get the cat."

"Good idea."

"Let's go get her before she does any more damage," said the doctor.

The jaguar had been contained in a most original and primitive way. Several animal keepers had rushed to the scene and were directed to bring trash can lids and rakes. They surrounded the animal, then yelled and beat the trash can lids whenever she attempted to leave the area. It looked like a scene more suited to India at the turn of the century than Los Angeles in the early seventies.

We began to prepare the tranquilizer dart, carefully measuring the proper dose to bring the jaguar down. The dangers of shooting her with the dart were as follows: 1) Big cats don't fall asleep right away. With the proper dosage, the drop time would be about five minutes. 2) A high percentage of the darts misfire and don't inject anything but fatty tissue. You have to wait quite a while before you can shoot again because the animal may have received a full dose that is seeping out of the deep layer of fat. 3) Some animals get very angry when you shoot them with a dart because it is a very large gauge needle and it causes a fair amount of pain.

Now it stands to reason that all of these things are much more significant when the animal is outside the cage. She would be inclined to attack someone, most likely the one who had shot her with the rifle. That would be me. To be very honest, my mouth was dry, my heart was pounding, and I was shaking so hard that I wished someone would adjust my vertical hold. I raised the gun to my shoulder and began to zero in on the most muscular area of her hindquarters. She looked at me and I stopped breathing for a second. I would pull the trigger when she looked away.

The silence was shattered by the arrival of our assistant director, Dr. Nathan Gale.

"Don't shoot!" he yelled with firm authority.

I lowered the gun and he joined us for a brief conference.

"Listen guys, she just wants back in her cage. If we shoot her and the dart misfires she might run for the hills. If she gets loose in Griffith Park it might take a week to find her. The police would want her shot and we don't want that. Let's just apply gentle pressure and guide her back to her cage. When she sees the open door she'll run in."

I repeated an axiom to myself, "The boss may not always be right, but the boss is always the boss." Then I said, "Gee, it's worth a try. We haven't got anything to lose." I hoped I sounded less skeptical than I felt.

Dr. Gale had a couple of keepers run ahead and open the door to her cage. He organized the rest of us into two lines so that we formed a corridor through which she would walk. Then he took the dangerous position. He began to slowly put pressure on her by moving closer and closer. She snarled and swiped but he stood his ground. Finally she began to move. He applied constant and even pressure, not enough to challenge her but not so little that she would stop. It went so smoothly that it began looking like a man out for a walk with his pet jaguar. But the most difficult moment was still ahead. Would she go easily through the door to her cage? Not only did she go easily; she actually became excited and ran to get back in her cage. This defied reason and logic. Something inside of me had told me that she wanted her freedom, and that hadn't turned out to be the case at all.

I couldn't help but admire Dr. Gale's courage, but I was more intrigued with how he seemed to know how the jaguar would respond when she saw her cage. So I asked Dr. Gale, "How did you know what she would do?"

His answer was great. "Well, you never really know for sure what a wild animal will do and that's why we call them wild. But you can make a good guess based on Heine Hediger's book, *Psychology and Behavior of Animals in Zoos and Circuses*. Hediger's thesis is that an animals perspective changes as soon as he leaves his territory or home—his cage, if you will. He quickly senses that he has nowhere to run. He has no sense of his surroundings; to him it's unfamiliar territory. He becomes insecure. Home represents security, so it becomes the desired destination."

"Would this method always be the best choice?" I questioned.

"I stay away from 'always' answers, but I do believe it would usually be the best method to try first."

We humans are not so different from the jaguar. I remembered back to my own childhood when I had decided to run away. My mother had spanked me for some justifiable reason and I became indignant. I announced that I was going to run away and she offered to help me pack. She even made an excellent lunch for me. I stood by as she neatly folded my clothes and laid them in the suitcase. She snapped it closed and handed it to me along with the lunch bag. We walked together, she and I, to the end of our driveway. I looked first to the right and then to the left. The world seemed bigger and more threatening than I had remembered it and my eyes filled with tears. I began to sob and my mother asked kindly what was making me cry.

"I don't know where to go!" I wailed.

"Would you like to go home?" she said.

"Yes."

"You know that means you'll have to be good, don't you?"

"Yes." (My mother would believe anything.)

She let me come home, and feelings of relief and security welled up from the deep within my five-year-old soul.

Have you read the story of the Prodigal Son recently? It may be found in the fifteenth chapter of the Gospel of Luke. The son becomes increasingly unhappy in the faraway country and he begins to long for home. Home represents the presence of his father, and he senses that the proper attitude is humility and subjection. The father's response is affection and complete acceptance. We must never forget that the father always loved the son, even when the son was in the faraway country. Let us also never forget that the son was not allowed to perform any nonsense at all underneath the roof of the father. Peace and security are reserved for those who keep their mind on the Lord.

> Open the gates
> That the righteous nation which keeps faith
> May enter in.
> Thou dost keep him in perfect peace,
> Whose mind is stayed on thee,
> Because he trusts in thee.
> Trust in the LORD for ever
> For the LORD GOD
> Is an everlasting rock.
> Isaiah 26:2–4

My friend, if you're home, stay home. If you're not, come home. There was an occasion when Jesus offended many who had been following Him. The Bible tells us that many withdrew and stopped walking with Him. "Jesus said to the twelve, 'Do you also wish to go away?' Simon Peter answered him, 'Lord, to whom shall we go? You have the words of eternal life.'" (John 6: 67–68)

In the words of J.B. Coats' hymn, "Where could I go but to the Lord?"

CHACA, UH UH...

The phone range and my first thoughts were, "Who died?" Why else would anybody call at 12:05 a.m. other than to tell you somebody had died?

"Hello," I answered. This better be really good or really bad, I thought.

"Richmond, how would you like a little adventure in your life?" I recognized the voice of my boss, the zoo's young but very capable veterinarian.

"Sure, what's up?"

"The police just called. They want us to catch a killer ape that's loose in Highland Park. Meet me at the zoo in a few minutes."

As I hung up the phone I found myself wishing he had not said "killer ape." Of course, if a killer ape were loose in Highland Park it would need our help. That was a rough neighborhood.

I pushed my car to its limits and the freeway lights and signs charged at me like an onslaught of wooden soldiers. They briefly appeared in my rear-view mirror and quickly faded from view. As I drove, I made an inventory of what we might need in the capture of the killer ape. Tranquilizer gun, nets, ropes and assorted drugs. My damp palms gripped the steering wheel, and I wondered if my boss would notice if I didn't show up. I was probably the only one he called, so I concluded he might.

I skidded around the freeway off-ramp and entered the zoo's immense parking lot. Waiting at the entrance to the zoo was a black and white police car, its blue and amber lights pulsating with anticipation. Two officers were sitting in the front seat.

"Your boss is already at the health center. He wanted us to bring you up." I jumped in the back of the police car and we screamed past the security guard who was manning the gate. "Killer ape, huh?" I asked.

"Tore up his master real good. Went after one of our officers, too. That ape is one mean son of a gun." (The officer didn't exactly say "son of a gun.") "One of our guys discharged his revolver at it, but he missed. We'll get the sucker, though."

By the time we pulled up to the zoo health center, Dr. Bill Hulsizer had already gathered everything we would need. We threw it in their trunk and jumped into the back seat. The car lurched forward, and in no time we were on the freeway with siren howling. We passed several cars, all of which looked as though they were standing still. I glanced at the speedometer and noticed that we were going ninety miles an hour.

I turned towards Bill and asked, "So what do you think we're up against?"

He was the scientific type and would not speculate. He shrugged his shoulders and said, "We'll see."

I have always suffered from an over-active imagination, and it wouldn't have surprised me if King Kong himself stepped on the police car when we got there. We flew down the off-ramp and wove our way deep into a residential area. It looked as though we had entered a war zone. The officers were stopped by a crusty sergeant who pointed into the night and said, "They're waitin' for you at the command post."

"Command post," I said with a tinge of sarcasm in my voice. "What did you get us into, Doctor?"

"We'll see," he said with a wry smile. Boy sometimes those scientific types can really make you mad.

There were police cars everywhere. All of them had their lights flashing on and off, and all of the neighbors were clustered in small groups, discussing the crisis. We arrived at the command post, and an officer with plenty of authority called for a mass meeting. Officers began showing up from everywhere. I'm sure there were more than fifty. We were brought to the center of the group and the officer with all the authority said, "Men, this is Dr. Bill Hulsizer and his assistant Gary Richmond. These guys are experts from the zoo. They're going to help us track down the ape." He turned to us and said, "You guys are in charge. What do you want us to do?"

Bill and I looked at each other and I think we both wanted to laugh. Bill was the shy type. He was a very competent veterinarian, but there was no way he was going to order around the policemen that surrounded us. I didn't want to usurp his authority so I waited for him to make the first move. He put his arm on my shoulder and said, "Gary is the capture expert. Let's let him take charge."

"Take it," said the man with the biggest badge. So I did.

"Is there anybody here who has actually seen the animal we are after?" I probed.

A young officer stepped forward and said, "I did, sir."

"Can you describe him for us?"

"The light wasn't too hot. He was big, though. I discharged my revolver at him, but I believe I missed. Scared the heck out of me." (The officer didn't exactly say "heck.")

"Is the owner around here or any neighbors who have seen the animal? It would really be helpful if we knew what we were after."

The owner's father was brought to us, and as it turned out, he was the man who had been attacked. Most of his upper body was bandaged, including his face. The owner was in jail on several counts, all having to do with possessing or selling narcotics. It seems that he had developed a drug habit in Vietnam and brought it home with him. That's not all he brought with him. He also brought home a young pet that grew up to be something very large and very dangerous. I asked the man if he had a photograph of his son's pet. He said he did and reached for his wallet. As he handed me the picture he explained how he had sustained his injuries. It seems that while his son was in jail the responsibility of feeding the creature was his. The creature only liked the son, and attempting to get food into the cage was a daily act of courage. This was the night the father lost the battle. Blood was seeping through his gauze bandages, and I could just feel the tension building among the officers. I studied the photograph and was somewhat relieved to discover that the "killer ape" was really just a large monkey. It was a stump-tailed macaque—a very large specimen with two-inch canines.

I addressed the father once more, "Is there anything the monkey likes?" I was thinking of a favorite food item and was unprepared for the man's answer.

He was a Mexican-American gentleman and said with great enthusiasm, "Chaca likes it when you say, 'Chaca, Uh Uh.' I don't know why, but it calms him down." I thanked him very much for his help and began to speak to the assembly of policemen.

"Officers, I have very good news for you. We are not after a killer ape but a very large monkey named Chaca. Chaca is not the kind of animal that you would need to shoot, and frankly, I will not help you look for him if I have to worry about getting shot. If it would make you feel better, carry your night sticks. The owner's father has just told me that their pet likes it when you say, 'Chaca, Uh Uh,' so I suggest that as you go through the neighborhood you repeat that phrase over and over. We will wait here until he is sighted then we will take over. He is most likely scared to death after being shot at and is simply hiding."

As the officers spread out, Dr. Hulsizer leaned over to me and said, "Gary, it's not going to do any good for them to be saying 'Chaca, Uh Uh.'"

"It will, too. It will keep them calm. If they think they're helping their own cause they might not shoot each other." Than Bill and I got the giggles as Los Angles' finest went from house to house and from garage to garage saying, "Chaca, Uh Uh."

A police helicopter thundered overhead and turned on its blinding searchlight. Backyards were bathed in light, and although it was 2:00 a.m. we had the passing sensation of walking about in broad daylight. Walkie-talkies crackled and squeaked as policemen checked in to report that they had not sighted Chaca. The helicopter search was finally called off, and we again heard the masculine chant, "Chaca, Uh Uh...Chaca, Uh Uh." It sounded like a soundtrack from an old jungle movie and it would have fit the moment if someone had said, "The natives are getting restless."

At 2:45 a.m., an officer came running up to us and announced that his partner had Chaca cornered in a garage. We grabbed our equipment and hurried to the site. Most of the policemen were already there. They parted to let us through so that we might enter the side door of the garage. When we got inside, we saw Chaca huddled under a small fishing boat which was sitting snugly on its boat trailer. Chaca was protecting his face from the bright beam of light that issued forth from the sergeant's blue-steel flashlight. Chaca's body language was screaming, "Don't shoot, please don't shoot!"

His capture was not in the least dramatic. We laid a net over his trembling body and he fell over. I believe he was very near to fainting. We transferred Chaca to a travel cage and took him back to the zoo. He was kept there for thirty days in quarantine to determine whether or not he was carrying any transmissible diseases. He was then moved to another facility and we never saw him again.

It was after 4:00 a.m. when I crawled back into bed. It had been a great adventure and one with a happy, injury-free conclusion. I was clearly one of the most memorable experiences of my entire life. I cannot recall any deliberate thought concerning God during the whole night. But He was there, caring, protecting. And I can't prove it, but I think He was laughing. One of the most comforting thoughts that I have ever entertained is from a quote by Ruth Harm Calkins from her classic book of poems, *Tell Me Again Lord, I Forget.*

> Love me as you do,
> You understand so well,
> That when I want you least
> I need you most.*

You see, even when I am not thinking of Him, He is thinking of me. It is then that He comes to me and in my weakness His strength is made perfect.

If you want to get a feel for the depth of this truth then put down this book and read the Book of Esther. It is the only book in the Bible that never mentions God in any way. Nothing supernatural is mentioned. But from the first to the last page God is there, developing the character of a beautiful woman and protecting His people.

---

*From *TELL ME AGAIN, LORD, I FORGET* by Ruth Harms Calkins. Published by Tyndale House Publishers, Inc. ©1986. Used by permission.

Easy to Grab, Hard to Let Go

Don't you just hate king cobras? I know I do—and I came by my feeling honestly. Our zoo had a thirteen-foot giant that seemed to me to be the embodiment of evil. He had a scar over his left eye that made him look mean and, more significantly, kept him from shedding his skin in a normal fashion. At least twice a year we would get the dreaded phone call from the reptile house: "The cobra shed his skin last week, but the eye cap didn't come off. Looks infected. Suppose you and the doc could come down and clean it?"

A snake's skin includes a clear scale over the eye to protect it from sand and foreign objects. Snakes have no eyelids, so they have no way to blink for protection. The snake's scar prevented a normal shed, so the eye cap needed to be surgically removed.

We made the appointment for the next day. Arrangements were more critical for this procedure because of its extreme danger. Only two people at the zoo could take responsibility for grabbing the more deadly snakes, and this was the most deadly. This snake's venom glands contain enough poison to kill five hundred adults—a fact that seemed to come up every time we did this procedure.

The curator of reptiles was assigned to grab the head, and two reptile keepers were to steady the body. When the snake was subdued, the veterinarian would begin the delicate surgery. His arena kept him inches from a lethal injection. My job was to furnish the scalpel, sponge, hemostat, and anything else to expedite the procedure.

The capture of the cobra was as follows: The five of us took our positions. The two keepers stood on either side of the large cage door. The curator stood in front of the door about six feet away. The vet and I stood on either side of the curator about ten feet from the door. The keepers' only defense were sheer bird nets with two-foot handles.

With a nod of his head, the curator signaled for the door to be opened. Seconds later the king cobra appeared. As soon as he saw us, he stopped, spread his hood, and raised to full stature. The cage was two feet off the ground, so we were all looking at the snake at eye level. The cobra was trembling with excitement as he, in turn, stared at each of his five enemies. He seemed to be choosing who would be his prey. The curator was chosen, and with shocking quickness the snake lunged forward, hissing and growling with malevolent rage. With lightning speed, the skilled keepers placed the sheer nets over the snake's head. And as he pushed to get through the curator firmly grasped his neck just behind his venom sacs. The keepers grabbed the writhing body, then the curator nodded and said, "Let's get this over with."

The pressure was incredible. The vet's hands were trembling and beads of sweat began to run down the curator's forehead. The curator turned to me and said, "Do you have any cuts or scratches on your hands?"

I looked and said, "No."

"Get a wad of paper towels, quick," he followed in a strained voice. I did so.

"Now, put it in the cobra's mouth."

The king watched the paper towels as they were carefully positioned to allow him to bite them. He bit down violently and began to chew. The towels became yellow with venom until they began to drip.

The curator continued, "Did you know several Indian elephants die every year from king cobra bites? A man could never survive a bite with a full load of venom. That's why I'm having you drain his venom sacs. My hands are sweaty and my fingers are cramping."

The curator looked sheet white, exhausted, as if he were going to faint. His lips had a blue tinge and his voice was weak. The cobra continued to struggle to twist free and its deadly fangs, clearly visible, were stretching to find a thumb or wrist to puncture. I wasn't sure the curator could complete the task.

The vet said, "Finished!" Then the three men holding the thirteen-foot giant backed toward the cage. They put in the tail, then the mid-body, leaving the curator to put in the neck and head. He turned to us for just a second and said with a strained voice, "Cobras are easy to grab, but hard to let go." He threw the snake into the cage and a keeper slammed the door shut. We had survived the procedure. If I live to be a hundred, I will never forget his words: "Cobras are easy to grab, but hard to let go."

There are many situations in life that are parallels—easy to grab, but hard to let go—so it pays to think twice before you grab them. Indebtedness, vengeance, lying, adultery, drugs, alcohol, pornography, promiscuity, materialism, greed, jealously, envy, apathy, spiritual pride, complaining, hate—all these and many more are serpents that will drain your strength and bit you to death while you're trying to let them go.

There is a way which seems right to a man, but its end
is the way of death.

Proverbs 14:12

Samson found that embracing Delilah was easy and exciting. But his life was destroyed after he laid his head on her lap. Reread his story in chapters 13–16 of the Book Judges. Ask yourself two questions:

1. "Who do I know who has his head on Delilah's lap?" If you know someone who does, attempt a rescue.

2. "If I woke up on Delilah's lap, would there be anyone to rescue me?" If not, make the type of friend who would try.

FREE AS A BIRD

It didn't make sense to me. The criminals were as free as a bird and the birds were in jail. It probably doesn't make sense to you either. Let me explain.

When I first transferred to the zoo health center, I found myself caring for a cage full of red-tailed hawks. There were fifteen of them, and they were crowded together in a pitifully small cage. To my eye, they looked to be very depressed. I inquired as to the reason why we might be caring for fifteen red-tailed hawks off exhibit and the answer really frosted me.

The senior keeper, an extremely jovial Mexican-American man by the name of Johnny Torres, said, "Eeeeeh, those hawks are evidence for court trials. These guys caught them illegally and we keep them here until their trial is over."

"What happens when the court trials are over?" I asked.

"I don't know," he answered. "We never hear. Some of these birds have been here a long time. We don't even know which bird goes with what trial. So they'll probably die here."

"That doesn't make sense to me," I protested.

"Richmond, did somebody lie to you and tell you things make sense around here? It's best not to ask too many questions about this either. The guys down below, down in administration, they don't like to know that they got problems. So my advice is to drop it."

Well, to tell you the truth, it just wasn't in my nature to drop it. After all, it was the sixties and this was a cause. It seemed to me that the poor, the children and the animals needed help, and this was injustice pure and simple. The poachers were free and the poachees were being punished.

I inquired gently and became convinced that the birds were in trouble. Nobody cared about their plight, and the red tape to get them released was so sticky that no one would touch it.

There was really only one answer. They must be let go. But it must look like an accident. The punishment for letting low-risk animals out was nothing more than a notice to correct a deficiency. I had never received one before, but it would be a small price to pay to right this wrong.

I decided that I would let them go on a Tuesday afternoon when the supervisors were at the animal health committee meeting. They would be out of the area for about two hours, more than enough time to accomplish my mission.

Tuesday came and the supervisors left the hospital area. I made my way out to the cage, slipped the lock out of the hasp, and left the door wide open. I looked around. There was no one in sight. I slipped back into the health center and set about my duties with a profound send of fulfillment, an abiding feeling of satisfaction. It was not to last.

After one hour I decided to check the cage. Astonishment, disbelief, wonder and confusion reigned supreme as I beheld all fifteen birds still in the cage relaxing. There was still time. Perhaps the red-tails just needed some inspiration. Well, I know what would be inspirational. I ran into their cage waving my arms and growled like a bear. That inspired them, all right. They flew out of the cage and landed not ten feet from the cage door. The look that they gave me was pitiful. They were confused and it was clear to me that they wanted back into the cage. "Don't you see the sky?" I pleaded. "That's what you were meant for." I began feeling a little self-conscious inside the cage so I stepped out to finish my address. "What's wrong with you? You're not chickens. You're majestic birds of prey. You hunt your foot. God gave you a purpose, now go and fulfill it." I decided to go back to the health center. Maybe their instincts would take over and they would feel some primal urge to command the wind. I left for fifteen minutes and then returned. Not one bird had felt any urges. In fact, most had walked back into the cage. With fifteen minutes to go, I gave up. I don't mind telling you I was more than a little deflated. I ended up herding the few birds back into the cage like goats. Where had I gone wrong?

I had approached their problem anthropomorphically, which is a fancy way of saying I was projecting my thoughts into the minds of the birds. The birds had not been sitting in the cage longing to be free. Those were my thoughts. They had long since become satisfied with just waiting to be fed. No famines to suffer. No droughts to survive. No territorial battles to enjoin. It wasn't all bad, I felt bad, but they didn't. The reason I felt bad was because by caging them we had taken something from them that they needed to be noble—their purpose. God had created the red-tailed hawks to hunt rodents and reptiles. Few birds can equal their elegant flight or fearless pursuit of prey. This group of birds had been robbed of their ecological purpose. And we weren't even letting the zoo patrons appreciate them. That's what was bothering me.

I thought a bit more about freedom as I finished my responsibilities that day. I concluded that freedom was the ability to fulfill the purpose for which you were created. I further reasoned that man had an interesting distinction. Unlike the animals, man can never be kept from fulfilling his purpose. He is always and in every circumstance free to perform the function for which he was created. Man's purpose is to love and to serve God. The more difficult the circumstances, the greater the opportunity to achieve that purpose. The Apostle Paul, John Bunyan and Dietrich Boenhoeffer all wrote books that changed the world from jail cells. No one took their freedom from them. We are now and will always be free to be what we were meant to be, that creature designed to glorify God and enjoy Him forever.

Solomon, the wisest man that ever lived, put it this way:

> The end of the matter; all has been heard. Fear God, and keep his commandments; for this is the whole duty of man. For God will bring every deed into judgment, with every secret thing, whether good or evil.
> Ecclesiastes 12:13–14

The apostle Paul shares in Galatians 5:1:

> For freedom Christ has set us free...

In verse 13 he further states:

> For you were called to freedom, brethren; only do not use your freedom as an opportunity for the flesh, but through love be servants of one another.

Are you fulfilling the purpose for which you were created? Or have you become satisfied with the ways of the world? You have the freedom...now choose to be free.

You'd Better Sit Down

I was preparing a surgical pack in the zoo's well-stocked operating room when I was called to the phone. "Richmond, I hear the vets are at a conference and won't be back until this afternoon." I recognized the voice of the senior keeper at the children's zoo.

"That's right, Bill. Is something up?"

"Yeah! We have these raccoon kittens down here and they are both showing signs of losing the use of their hind legs. It's the darndest thing. We've never seen anything like this."

"Would you like me to pick them up? I could keep them up here until the vets get back from the conference. They will probably need to do some testing and take X-rays anyway."

"That would be great, Richmond. Then if they have something hot they won't be passing it around down here. Let's go for it."

I drove right down and picked them up. It was about 9:30 in the morning. I took them out of their carrying cage when I got back to the health center and confirmed that they were indeed losing the use of their hind legs.

Raccoon kittens are extremely appealing. These had been hand-raised and were both very playful and affectionate. They seemed all right except for the extreme weakness in their hind legs, so I placed them in the two large pockets of my lab coat. As I puttered from room to room I played with the little bandits. They loved to chew on my fingers and wrestle with my hands. But they soon tired and napped a good deal more than normal. When they woke they refused to eat and played a bit less enthusiastically than they had in the morning. I felt sorry for them so I stayed in contact with them the whole day long.

It was about four o'clock when the veterinarians returned. Dr. Bill Hulsizer came in first. He found me in the X-ray room. The color drained from his face when he saw the raccoon kittens in my pockets.

"Are they losing the use of their legs?" he asked in a most serious tone.

"How'd you know? You haven't even looked at them," I declared in genuine astonishment.

He lifted the young raccoons out of my pockets and placed them in a stainless steel cage onto a bath tower. "You'd better sit down, Gary. You're not going to be too happy about what I'm about to tell you."

I sat down wondering what I had done wrong. I couldn't think of anything, but that didn't stop me from wondering.

He looked me right in the eye and said, "I'm about 90 percent sure both the kittens have rabies."

"What?" I exclaimed in disbelief. "How could you know? You haven't even examined them."

Bill began to tell me a story that surprised and hurt me very much. He shared that our other veterinarian, Dr. Westfall, had given the raccoon kittens a modified live rabies vaccine as what she thought should be a standard procedure to protect them. She did not realize that, even though it prevents rabies in dogs, such a vaccine can cause rabies in raccoons. Bill said that he had discovered this serious error while he was reviewing the medical records at the children's zoo. He had confronted Dr. Westfall immediately, and she was very embarrassed about her lack of knowledge. She insisted that she would handle the situation her own way and asked Bill to back off as if he didn't know a thing. Unfortunately, that's exactly what he did. She discovered a statistic that indicated that there was a 50% chance the raccoons would not come down with rabies at all, so she decided to play the odds. She even went as far as erasing the medical records at the children's zoo. Both vets checked the raccoons two to three time a day, but they never mentioned anything to me. They didn't count on the raccoons coming down with rabies the one day that they were both away at a conference.

"How can you be sure they have the disease?" I challenged. "They're not foaming at the mouth."

"They have the more common symptoms. What we call the mute form of the disease."

"Does this mean that I will have to go through the series of shots that I've always heard about?" I asked.

"That depends on whether or not you have experienced vital contact. If you have been bitten or your skin has been broken or scratched, that is vital contact. If you had any open sores that their saliva might have entered, that would be vital contact. In the case of the baby raccoons, it would be considered vital if they so much as scratched you because these little guys put their paws in their mouths so much. Let's see your hands."

My hands were covered with nicks and scratches, about half of which they had caused that day. Bill nodded and said, "I think you'll want to take the treatment."

I felt sick. I would now be finding out if the treatment was worthy of its horrible reputation.

The raccoon kittens were sacrificed and their brains were sent to two different labs for analysis. Both labs confirmed rabies. A thorough investigation was launched to determine who might have sustained vital contact with the raccoons. One hundred and twenty people had been exposed, but only five in a vital way. There were two children's zoo attendants, the zoo's photographer and his assistant, and me. One of the children's zoo attendants refused to take the treatment for personal reasons, so as it turned out only four of us met to take the hard road together.

Forty hours after exposure we were driven to County General Hospital. The first matter of business was to determine if we were strong enough to endure the treatment. They gave each of us a thorough physical, and we all proved to be of sound body. Then they told us that 3 percent of the people who took the treatment died from it. Of course each of us thought we might be in that 3 percent, and one of us was nearly correct.

We were given other statistics that spelled out our chances. If we were punctured by a rabid animal there was a fifty-fifty chance that we would come down with the disease. If we came down with the disease, there was a 100 percent chance that we would die from it if we didn't take the treatment. We were also warned that one out of four of us might experience a violent allergic reaction to the massive dose of horse serum we were about to receive.

Then the treatment began. They decided that my dose of horse serum would be fifty cc's. The syringe and needle looked like an outlandish prop from a bizarre comedy, but let me assure you that it was not funny. I hope I shall never receive that large a dose of anything ever again. I hurt tremendously, and sitting down was out of the question for hours to come.

They led us into another room and we began the series to the abdominal area. They chose that area because we use the least amount of muscles there. Rabies shots, in addition to being painful, are also somewhat complicated. First, a map is drawn to direct where the doctor will administer the shots. He writes the numbers one through twenty-three right on the abdomen in indelible ink. That way he will not give the shots in the same place twice. The shots are carefully administered subcutaneously (between the muscles and the skin). Then the swelling begins and the severe soreness sets in.

Shots one and two were given. They were very painful. The burning pain lasted about two minutes and gave way to soreness and intense itching. But it was bearable, and we began to encourage each other during each administration.

We met at the zoo every morning and were driven to the hospital. The hospital is not an architectural triumph, and it resides in a depressed area of Los Angeles. It seemed grey, gloomy, and institutional, especially stark after leaving the gardenlike atmosphere of the zoo in Griffith Park.

The four of us became good friends and determined that we ought to make the best of a bad thing. We would all take turns pretending to foam at the mouth and trying to bite one of the others. I shared that this experience would be great to tell our grandchildren in years to come—it may even make a good story for a book someday. When I discovered that my blood was going to be valuable and could be sold after I completed the treatment, I was overjoyed. Karen, the children's zoo attendant that was with us, said, "Gary, you're making this sound like we have just had one big stroke of luck. It's not that good," she added.

Karen was not at the zoo to meet us for our fifth day of treatment. She had been admitted to the hospital the night before. So after we received our ninth and tenth shots, we went up to her room to see her. She was covered with a fiery red rash and her face was very puffy. We managed to cheer her up some, but all of us were finding it hard to be good little soldiers. The course of treatment was making us all tired. I had a constant headache and was nauseous most of the time. We were all experiencing a good deal of swelling and itched fiercely all the time. The doctors said that these symptoms were good signs. It meant that our bodies were fighting the virus. I know my body was fighting back, but I wished it was not the battleground as well.

I was not up to working on the sixth day and my wife, Carol, insisted on driving me straight to the hospital. On the way my fingers began to swell and hives began to appear everywhere. The doctors were a bit concerned, but they felt that the symptoms could be controlled with medication. So they let me go home.

A few hours later Carol drove me back to County General, and they admitted me quickly. The medication hadn't helped at all.

I was becoming very ill with a ravaging case of serum sickness. The swelling progressed until I was unrecognizable. I couldn't bend my fingers and it was painful to touch anything. The itching was fiery and incredible. No pain that I have ever encountered before or since compares to the sensations that I felt during that twenty-four hours of hell. I felt trapped in the dimensions of my own body. There is not a torture chamber on earth that could have punished me more severely. It was difficult to breathe, and I was racked with nausea and retching constantly. I stayed coherent during the whole ordeal and saw the concerned look on the doctors' faces in the intensive care unit. I knew that I was in trouble and prayed constantly for relief. I repeated the name of Jesus over and over and asked Him for strength. I felt His presence with me.

I thought that I might be dying and I was afraid. I wasn't so afraid for myself, but I didn't want to leave Carol alone with our two little girls, Marci and Wendi. I begged the Lord to make the feelings go away, but they didn't. I watched the hospital clock from my position on the gurney. Minutes seemed like hours, and hours seemed like years. It got to a point where the pain was so intense that I lost my resolve to live. I prayed, "Take me, Lord, and I'll trust You to take care of my family." I really wanted to die, but still the night went on. I tried to think of the great saints and remembered Job. His trials lasted nearly a year, and he had continued to hang in there. I remembered Jeremiah who had come to the end and proclaimed that the Lord was his sufficiency. Then I remember the apostle Paul and what he had written to the church at Philippi:

> ...that I may know Him and the power of His resurrection, and may share His sufferings, becoming like Him in His death...
>
> Philippians 3:10

A tremendous peace settled in as I realized I had been given a chance to know Christ in a different way than I had ever known Him before. He had suffered because of my sin, and now I was suffering because of someone else's sin. We had something in common now, and it helped me to know something about His powers of love that added to His greatness. He chose to suffer for me before I had loved Him in any way. There were only a handful of people I would be willing to suffer for, and all of them already loved me. How different Jesus was from me. How better. How perfect.

I resigned to the will of Jesus and He waited there with me.

I asked to talk to my wife in case it would be the last time I would get the chance. I was getting weaker by the minute. I told her that I wanted her to know that I loved her. She knew something was probably really wrong because I tend not to say that nearly as much as I should.

By morning there was a blessed relief that let me know that I was going to live. I thanked the Lord.

Dr. Westfall never apologized for her actions which almost cost us our lives, but I still forgave her gladly and freely because of what Jesus taught me during our night of horrors together.

> Therefore, since we are justified by faith, we have peace with God through our Lord Jesus Christ. Through him we have obtained access to this grace in which we stand, and we rejoice in our hope of sharing the glory of God. More than that we rejoice in our sufferings, knowing that our sufferings produce endurance, and endurance produces character, and character produces hope, and hope does not disappoint us, because God's love has been poured into our hearts by the Holy Spirit which has been given to us.
>
> Romans 5:1–5

Now that's Good News.

LADYBUG

When I was seven our family obtained a small black and tan puppy and named her Ladybug. I do not recall where we got her, but even after four decades have come and gone I can vividly recall the warmth of her head lying across my bare feet or the look of love in her eyes as she watched to see if she would be invited on any adventure that led her beyond the boundaries of our yard. She was an ardent traveler and loved to ride in the car. No dog ever born enjoyed more the wind whipping her ears and flapping her lips as she leaned as far as we would permit out the back window of our '53 Chevrolet station wagon.

She weighed in at about fifteen pounds, maybe twenty, and the consensus was that she was a cross between a cocker spaniel and a beagle.

Ladybug was a happy dog and ticklish. If you scratched her in just the right place she actually smiled. Now, I know that's hard to believe. If you saw it you would call it that, too.

When I was young I actually thought of her as a member of the family. She was the youngest child. To me she was Ladybug Richmond. She slept with us, and many was the morning that I was licked awake. Between the ages of seven and nine I never washed my ears because Ladybug did it for me almost every night.

She did have a fault that remained with her all the days of her life. She had breath that you could see on a warm day. Whatever doggy breath is, she had twice as much as should be allotted. We had to apologize for it more than once. She was also possessed of a great capacity for natural gas production and could not contain it.

Ladybug was my friend and shadow, and I always loved her but never more than one summer day that I asked for and obtained her forgiveness. Here is what happened.

I was raised in Altadena, California, a small friendly town nestled against the San Gabriel Mountains. You have seen these very mountains if you have watched the Rose Parade or the Rose Bowl Game. The San Gabriels watch over Pasadena and Altadena and most of the Los Angeles basin. Now Altadena had much to commend it, but right up there at the top, smack dab in the middle of the "amen corner" was Kern's Delicatessen. Old Mr. Kern had located some of the finest culinary delights known to the palates of our species. His Swiss cheese, pumpernickel bread, and kosher dill pickles were the best. It was a four-block walk to the deli, but I would make the walk anytime some benefactor would finance the pilgrimage.

One very hot summer afternoon in deep August I had a little extra cash and remembered how much I enjoyed biting into one of Mr. Kern's renowned kosher dills. I was with a friend, Doug Sigler, and asked if he would like to walk to Kern's with me. As it turned out, my brother and a friend of his decided to go also. When we got to the front door, Ladybug was wiggling with delight for she was sure we were going to let her come along. After a little banter, we agreed and were out the door on our way to the gates of heaven.

Ladybug was not leashed because she would never bite anyone. She was always bounding just ahead, stopping now and then to smell something and make a memory. She would run over and jump on us now and then to let us know she was glad to be part of the adventure. Ladybug was five going on six at the time, and I was going into the seventh grade in the fall.

When we arrived at Kern's, I purchased one piece of his pumpernickel bread, one slice of aged Swiss cheese, one large kosher dill pickle, and a bottle of Dad's Old Fashioned Root Beer. We had told Ladybug to sit at the front door and wait for us while we ate inside. Life doesn't get better than eating at Kern's Delicatessen with family and friends. We left only after licking our fingers clean, for leaving anything uneaten would have been a sin.

Once outside we ordered Ladybug to follow us home. Twenty steps down the street we looked into the Hillcrest Pharmacy window and noticed the second-ever issue of *Mad Magazine*. We again ordered Ladybug to sit on the sidewalk and wait for us while we went in the store. We all read *Mad Magazine* over my friend's shoulder and laughed at the absurd humor of the latest issue. Laughter's tears streamed down our faces. The store clerk asked us to buy or fly, so we left. We left a little embarrassed and a little miffed. We also left through the back door, which provided a shortcut home. We left Ladybug waiting patiently at the front door of Hillcrest Pharmacy.

On the way home we groused over being given the bum's rush. The afternoon began to blend with evening, and our friends both left for home and dinner. My dad came home from a hard day's work in construction and, after washing, up, called us to the dinner table. It was a meat and potatoes meal and had a lot of the kind of leftovers any family dog would kill for. My father scraped them onto a plate and stepped out the back door to call for Ladybug.

She didn't come. He asked Steve and me if we had seen her, and we both looked at each other. I didn't know for sure what

Steve was going to do, but I was trying to figure out a way to blame our thoughtless mistake on him. I refused to answer, hoping that if my brother spoke first he would get most of the blame for losing our dog. Steve finally admitted that we had left her outside the pharmacy. My Dad had a disgusted look, which he administered pretty equally as I remember. He told us to jump in the car, and we backed out of our driveway a lot faster than usual. He didn't say much, but he did inquire if we had traded our brains for sawdust. We knew well that we better not answer that particular question. If we said no, we were smart-mouthing. If we said yes, we were smart-mouthing. So we both did what he wanted us to do; we looked guilty and stupid and kept quiet. Now I don't know what you're thinking, but I don't agree with the notion that there are no appropriate times for a tongue-lashing. God did it all the time to Israel, and Jesus did it to His disciples. Steve and I were getting less than we deserved, and I knew it even then.

My father knew enough about dogs to know that Ladybug was capable of following her own scent home, so he followed the route we had walked to the delicatessen. The farther we drove without seeing her the worse I felt. I had let down one of my best friends and I knew it. I had a lump in my throat as I began to picture my dog run over by a car or cringing in the back of a cage at the dog pound. We finally rounded the corner of Mariposa Lane and Lake Street and saw a small dark form curled into a ball by the front door of the pharmacy. Steve stuck his head out the window and yelled, "Here, girl."

His yell awoke her, and she bounced against the glass thinking we were still in the store. Steve left the car and picked her up.

I have never witnessed a more emotional reunion. Ladybug wiggled until I thought she would fall apart. She whined happily all the way home and licked every hand that came within a foot of her.

My father, happy about the outcome, said, "All's well that ends well, but don't you two ever let that happen to your dog again. I don't have to tell you all the bad things that could have happened to her, do I?" We nodded.

That night I asked Ladybug if she wanted to sleep with me. Her tail wagged as she ran ahead of me and jumped up on the bed. When I turned out the light, I called her to come close and I hugged her and told her how sorry I was to have let her down. She just kissed me and rolled over to have me scratch her tummy. I did that until we both fell asleep.

Ladybug was always anxious to forgive. Her only desire was that she be part of a family, our family, her family. The saying that dogs are man's best friends really isn't so far off in my experience.

You know what made me remember this story? I was reading the story of the prodigal son in the fifteenth chapter of Luke. It is my favorite story in the Bible. As I thought about the father in the story, I was impressed by how anxious he was to forgive and be reunited to his son. The story answers the question, "How does God feel when we are off blowing it?" He is simply longing and waiting for us to come to our senses and come home. He is always, as my dog was with my brother and me, glad for the reunion. If you have been away from God for awhile and want to know how He feels, read this. If you want to know what to do about it, follow the prodigal son's lead and come home just as he did. Read it for yourself:

> Then Jesus said, "A man had two sons. The younger son said to his father, 'Give me my share of the property.' So the father divided the property between his two sons. Then the younger son gathered up all that was his and left. He traveled far away to another country. There he wasted his money in foolish living.

He spent everything that he had. Soon after that, the land became very dry, and there was no rain. There was not enough food to eat anywhere in the country. The son was hungry and needed money. So he got a job with one of the citizens there. The man sent the son into the fields to feed pigs. The son was so hungry that he was willing to eat the food the pigs were eating. But no one gave him anything. The son realized that he had been very foolish. He thought, 'All of my father's servants have plenty of food. But I am here, almost dying with hunger. I will leave and return to my father. I'll say to him: Father, I have sinned against God and have done wrong to you. I am not good enough to be called your son. But let me be like one of your servants.' So the son left and went to his father.

"While the son was still a long way off, his father saw him coming. He felt sorry for his son. So the father ran to him, and hugged and kissed him. The son said, 'Father, I have sinned against God and have done wrong to you. I am not good enough to be called your son.' But the father said to his servants, 'Hurry! Bring the best clothes and put them on him. Also, put a ring on his finger and sandals on his feet. And get our fat calf and kill it. Then we can have a feast and celebrate! My son was dead, but now he is alive again! He was lost, but now is found!' So they began to celebrate."

Luke 15:11–24

THE BEST CHIMP I HAVE EVER KNOWN

I will never forget Charlie. As chimps go, he was the best. Charlie was the dominant chimp of our collection and well loved by any whose privilege it had been to care for him. Charlie was a peacemaker.

The Los Angeles Zoo had eight chimps that formed a cohesive group. They were tight because they had a leader that didn't put up with any monkey business. Charlie spent a good deal of time keeping his group at peace, and that was no easy assignment. Toto and Jeanie were a part of his group. Toto was a former circus chimp and stirred up trouble whenever he could. He would often hoot and scream and charge his cage mates. He would then slap them with the back of his hand and run away. Then Toto would make dramatic and threatening gestures, and that's when Charlie would swing into action.

He was a little lighter than Toto but had long since established who was boss. Charlie would charge Toto and hold him down and scream at him. Toto would act submissive and Charlie would let him off the hook. In no time, Toto would be back to his old tricks, but Charlie never gave up on Toto. He tried his best, but Toto was a hopeless case.

Jeanie was no gift, either. She was always on the edge of a fit and very unpredictable. But Charlie was equal to all of his responsibilities. He was truly an exceptional chimpanzee.

One day a decision was made to remodel the very inadequate chimpanzee exhibit. It was also decided that the eight chimps would be kept at the health center until the remodeling was completed. We divided the group in half and placed them in adjacent cages. I can't remember whether there was much thought as to how we should divide them, but rational or not, our plan turned out to be a disaster.

Toto and Jeanie were housed with two of the young chimps in one cage while Charlie was housed with the coquettish Annie, the beautiful Bonnie, and the always affectionate Judy. It should have been heaven for Charlie to be separated from Toto, but that's not how it turned out.

The months began to pass, and Toto quickly realized that Charlie could do little more than yell at him from the next cage. Charlie would try his best to govern his group from the next cage, but it was futile. Charlie started to lose a little weight and began to show signs of depression. One morning, we found that our beloved group leader had died during the night. He died sitting up, leaning against the side of the cage nearest to Toto's group.

I cannot describe to you the sadness that descended over the health center. We felt as if we had lost a good friend. We had. He was the best chimp I have ever known.

When we performed a clinical examination, we were crushed by what we discovered. Charlie had died of a perforated ulcer. Things had been bothering him a lot more than he had been letting on. Not being able to keep his family at peace had taken a terrible toll on him.

One of the problems that a veterinarian encounters is the inability of his patients to tell him where it hurts so that they can be helped. If only Charlie could have let us know, we would have done anything to help him.

One of the advantages we have over the animal kingdom is that we can let somebody know we need help. We can point to where it hurts. We can ask for help.

God's Word speaks to us directly about asking for what we need.

> ...your Father knows what you need before you ask him
> Matthew 6:8

> Ask, and it will be given you; seek, and you will find; knock, and it will be opened to you. For every one who asks receives, and he who seeks finds, and to him who knocks it will be opened. Or what man of you, if his son asks him for bread, will give him a stone? Or if he asks for a fish, will give him a serpent? If you then, who are evil, know how to give good gifts to your children, how much more will your Father who is in heaven give good things to those who ask him!
> Matthew 7:7–11

> And whatever you ask in prayer, you will receive, if you have faith.
> Matthew 21:22

Have you asked the Lord for anything lately? You may ask for help if you are in trouble. You may ask for forgiveness if you have sinned. You may ask for gifts, like love for others, patience, or wisdom. You may even ask for God to help a close friend. He commands us to ask. It is His nature to want to help us. That is what being a Father is all about.

THE MAYOR IS COMING!

I came to dread the words "the mayor is coming." It wasn't that we were going to meet him. That would have been fun. Instead, it meant that we had to clean up the zoo in places where we didn't know we had places. We had to transform the zoo into an immaculate display for the mayor to see.

I remember once being made to clean up some building material behind an obscure barn in an obscure corner of the zoo. I offered my opinion that I didn't think the mayor would be coming behind this barn. The restroom facilities in the main zoo were perfectly acceptable.

My supervisor smiled. "Richmond," he said, "I'm paid to think. You are paid to do."

He must have been telling the truth, I thought, because I had never seen him do anything. I told him I didn't know what kind of money he made, but it must a thrill to be so overpaid for his responsibility.

He smiled again and pointed to the back of the barn and motioned for me to go there. So we shoveled and hosed and scrubbed and scoured until each section virtually gleamed with purity. And then we waited. And waited. And waited. Finally, the zoo closed for the day and well all went home exhausted and a little irritated.

But that is how it was. I can recall at least ten occasions when the mayor was announced and he never came. He did come to the front of the zoo one day, however, to have his picture taken with fifteen children from the Taiwanese community who were bussed in for a public relations shot. He gave a little speech about how he had been personally responsible for this marvelous zoo and then he kissed a child, sustaining the kiss until all had ample time to capture his benevolence. Then he walked away, completely unaware of the enormous manpower exerted on his behalf.

I inquired as to the possible reasons why he never actually came into the zoo, and was informed that he once had. Amazed, I asked what miracle had attracted him. Mark, one of our zoo's leading humorists, offered, "He must have caught the scent of cameras."

"It's the truth," offered another keeper. "He came to see the white rhinos, Sonny and Cher, let out for the first time. He made everybody wait until he arrived. When he got there he spent ten minutes looking for a place to stand where the television cameras would be sure to capture him when the rhinos made their first entrance. The mayor and his entourage climbed through wild roses and ankle deep ivy to stand on the hill just behind the exhibit. It turned out to be, as expected, the very best view for television. The mayor signaled the keeper to let the white rhinos out and filming began. Sonny snorted and pranced out in a thunderous manner, followed by his saucy mate. The crowd cheered and, as if trained, the rhinos stopped to consider their public right below the mayor. He couldn't have planned it better. But he did leave one important consideration to chance."

"What was that?" I asked in rapt attention.

"The automatic sprinklers," said the keeper, beginning to laugh hysterically. "They came on with a vengeance. The television news teams got it all. There were dignitaries running in every direction. They were soaked. It was great!"

"What did the mayor do?" I asked.

"He just left. I heard he was really bent out of shape. Anyway, I think that's why he doesn't come into the zoo anymore. He's probably still mad."

That story sort of made up for all the extra work we had to do, I thought.

In fairness, it occurred to me that perhaps we dreaded the mayor's "visits" because of the extra work. We might even have looked forward to his coming if we hadn't let things get so far behind. We shouldn't have let junk accumulate; there was no reason for it.

There is a King who will be coming and we have all been given notice. I'm sure you know that I am referring to the return of the Lord Jesus Christ. Many people have foolishly predicted the date, even though the Bible says that no man knows the time of His appearing. He will come unexpectedly, "like a thief in the night." And He will inspect us with an absolutely thorough review. Over and over the Bible cautions us to be ready, to prepare for His coming.

> ...there is laid up for me the crown of righteousness, which the Lord, the righteous judge, will award to me on that Day, and not only to me but also to all who have loved his appearing.
>
> 2 Timothy 4:8

The term "loved his appearing" has always intrigued me. That would be those who are ready and current in their walk with Jesus. The folks who have let a lot of waste material accumulate in their lives would dread the thought of His coming. How about it? Up to date? Or do you have some important cleaning to do in your life?

LADY TWINKLE TOES

I NEVER REALIZED

The arrival of a new rhinoceros at the Los Angeles Zoo turned out to be one of the most meaningful spiritual events in my life. Let me tell you about it.

One of the goals of a modern zoo is reproduction, especially of rare animals. This goal could not be realized with our black rhino collection because we owned only one male, Arthur. Arthur (King Arthur) was a young, robust, jaunty, temperamental male. But he needed a lady. We came through in a big way by our purchase of Lady Twinkle Toes, a dark, elusive beauty who pulsated with rhino charm.

She arrived at the zoo in a crate so large it could not be driven to the back of the exhibit because of the low bridges and tunnels that were a part of the back-road system. So the decision was made to lift the crate into the front of the exhibit with a large crane that stood waiting for her arrival. When she did arrive, it was clear she was very upset. Her trip from Africa had been miserable. She had encountered heavy seas in both the Atlantic and Pacific. Now, on the same day, she had been taken from the cargo hold of a ship in her crate, lifted onto a truck, and driven forty miles over the Los Angeles freeway system to the zoo. The variety of smells, sounds and shadows had taken their toll on an animal that is extremely subject to feat and anxiety. She was feeling progressively more trapped by the crate and she wanted out. NOW!

We knew this because she was frequently ramming the door of her massive crate so hard that we heard cracking and noticed splintering around the hinges. The order was shouted to hurry it up with the steel cables. There was a frenzy of activity as the cables were bolted together and attached to the giant hook at the end of the crane's cable. "Lift away!" The crate began to rise amidst hoorahs and the diesel roar that thundered from the crane. Billows of smoke belched forth from an engine that obviously needed more maintenance. Inside the crate Lady Twinkle Toes had long since reached her stress limit. She was possessed by terror, and in her mind her life was on the line. Her very survival was in question. Seventeen feet in the air, the crate began to rock violently. Four-by-fours bowed, cracked and fell to the ground as the door began to disintegrate before our eyes. The crane operator swung the crate into position as quickly as possible while the rhino, with incredible strength, blasted the last vestiges of the door off its hinges.

We were terrified. If she attempted to jump from that height, she would be crushed and killed by her own weight. Rhinos see very poorly, and she stared downward without the focus or intelligence to interpret her circumstances. She was trembling with fright and her eyes were filled with tears. Ten feet, eight feet, six feet, four feet. Still four feet above the ground, Lady Twinkle Toes opted for freedom. She fell with a sickening thud and we waited, with bated breath and clenched teeth, hoping she would be able to get up. She snorted and struggled successfully to a standing position. Her body was trembling violently with colossal fear, the kind that produces rage. She noticed a large boulder that through tear-filled eyes looked like a man or another animal. She charged it mightily. When she hit it, it moved only slightly and she fell to her knees. Staggering again to her feet, she noticed another boulder and charged it. Again the impact brought her to her knees. This time she got up a little more slowly. Then the most amazing thing happened…her whole body began to glisten red in the morning sun. She seemed to be perspiring great drops of blood from every pore in her body.

I turned to the veterinarian and exclaimed, "Doctor, what's going on? I have never seen anything like this before!"

"This animal has reached a maximum of stress," he said. "Rhinos, hippos, and elephants under this kind of stress can burst capillaries all over their bodies. She can't take much more stress. She's in great danger."

We were all glad when she stopped her awesome displays of fear and rage and began to calm down. As I considered this marvel, the words of another doctor, the beloved physician Luke, echoed in my mind.

> And being in agony, he (Jesus) prayed more earnestly; and his sweat became like great drops of blood falling down upon the ground.
> Luke 22:44

I thought, "Lord, I never realized. I never dreamed that You knew about stress in this way. How trapped You must have felt. How alone. You really can understand how I feel."

The Lord left us with two truths in this incident. It is good to reach out to friends during times of great stress; but when they don't come through, God is always sufficient. He will get us through. Jesus is into stress management. We read in Matthew 11:28–30:

> Come to me, all who labor and are heavy laden, and I will give you rest. Take my yoke upon you, and learn

from me; for I am gentle and lowly in heart, and you will find rest for your souls. For my yoke is easy, and my burden is light.

Are you stressed? Take it to the Counselor first. Jesus understands.

GOOD FOR SOMETHING

There is a dark side to my nature that I must confess. Let me do that for the sake of a clear conscience. You see, I take an abnormal pleasure from incidents involving pompous people being made to look ridiculous. This is hard to admit, but is very true and probably not very pastoral ("Vengeance is Mine," saith the Lord). Let me share a story that perhaps best illustrates the pinnacle of joy I am capable of attaining.

In the early 1970s, the Los Angeles Zoo hired a brand new curator of mammals. She had no previous zoo experience and had never worked with mammals. However, she did have a Ph.D., and someone in a high place felt that was more than enough. Her doctorate was related to reptiles and amphibians, and her thesis was a study of how the environment of Central American affected the evolution of frogs. She was clearly coming from a highly academic approach to life which left her, for the most part, on the outside looking in regarding the animal-keeping staff.

My first contact with her was very revealing. She stormed into the health center and said, "I want you to open that door and hold down that chimp. I need to see his ear tattoo." She pointed at Toto. Now Toto was a former circus chimp who had become psychotic. At a hundred and fifty pounds, he was six times as strong as a man and would never submit to this kind of restraint. I gave her the benefit of the doubt and said, "You are kidding, aren't you?"

She bristled, "I am not!"

"Doctor, no combination of ten men could hold down that chimp. But if you find ten willing men, I'll open the door for them."

She stormed out.

She formed a good friendship with my supervisor, the zoo veterinarian, and came to the health center often. She made it clear to him that the only location in the zoo she found intellectually stimulating was in his presence. I'm not sure how she pulled it off, but I always felt like a Quasimodo or an Igor when she came for her visits. The veterinarian would also change his attitude toward me. I felt like the lowly help, not his right-arm assistant, while she was there. So I made it a point to get lost whenever she showed up.

Her first major assignment was to send a medium-size black bear to the Paris Zoo. She designed a shipping crate and sent specifications to the maintenance crew for construction. On one of my journeys to Maintenance, I saw the nearly finished crate and inquired what it was for. I was told it was for the bear to go to Paris. It was one-inch plywood interlined with thin aluminum. I told the gentleman the bear would never leave the Los Angeles airport. He said he just built it to the specs; the curator had designed it. I saw her later that day and, in an effort to be helpful, said, "Doctor, the crate you had built will never leave LAX...the bear will tear it to pieces."

She looked at me as if I were a child and said, "I got my design from a book by a world authority on bears, and I'm quite confident this will do very nicely, thank you."

"I assure you, Doctor, the bear has never read the authority; and even if he had, he'd eat the crate anyway."

She stormed off.

When the day came, we tranquilized the bear and put him in the crate. We watched as the bear-laden truck headed for the airport. I left all the tranquilizing equipment in the Health Center truck on the strong hunch that I was right. The transport truck left at 10 a.m. and returned without the bear at noon. The keeper stayed only long enough to know that the bear was waking up from the tranquilizer. If we were called, it would be before 1 p.m., which was air-freight departure. I was wrong; it was 1:05 p.m. A frantic voice, angry and afraid, demanded that somebody get to the airport quick…the bear was chewing his way out of the crate. I grabbed an assistant, jumped into the truck, and arrived at the airport in less than forty minutes.

The air-freight terminal was completely locked down; all work had ceased. We saw one man start to wave his arms frantically when he saw the zoo truck. His first words were, "Quickly, quickly!" I grabbed the tranquilizing equipment and followed him into a side door. It led to an office where ten men were peering through a small window at a lone baggage cart in the middle of the massive air-freight building. The cart was rocking back and forth in the dim confines of the building. When my eyes focused, I saw the bear. He had one leg and one shoulder out of the crate. I could see him chewing small chunks of the crate and spitting them onto the baggage cart. He would be out in ten minutes. I loaded a syringe with an adequate dose of phencyclidine hydrochloride, walked into the terminal, and climbed onto the baggage cart. The bear—not a mean bear—looked at me as if to say, "Could you help me get out of here?" I gave him a quick shot in the shoulder, and he never even winced. He quickly fell asleep. The workers at air freight cheered, and after a quick look at the creature that had brought their world to a halt, they returned to work, now sadly behind schedule.

We loaded the bear and the demolished crate onto our truck and returned to the zoo. When we arrived we were met by the curator and a host of keepers who were getting a good laugh out of the whole incident. The bear was carried to his grotto while the curator fingered the shredded plywood and torn aluminum. Our eyes met briefly. I was hoping she would say something—anything—that would help me feel comfortable in her presence. She stormed off. But you could have sent an elephant in the next crate she had built.

I never learned to enjoy her company and have always taken more pleasure in that incident that I should. However, I did learn something from her. My father-in-law said best: "Everyone is good for something if only to serve as a bad example." I learned again how poor it is to treat people like dirt, to make them feel small and inadequate.

C.S. Lewis writes in *Mere Christianity*:

> In God you come up against something which is in every respect immeasurably superior to yourself. Unless you know God as that—and therefore, know yourself as nothing in comparison—you do not know God at all. As long as you are proud you cannot know God. A proud man is always looking down on things and people: and, of course, as long as you are looking down, you cannot see something that is above you.
> Luckily, we have a test. Whenever we find that our religious life is making us feel that we are good—above all, that we are better than someone else—I think we may be sure that we are being acted on, not by God, but by the devil. The real test of being in the presence of God is that you either forget about yourself altogether or see yourself as a small, dirty object. It is better to forget about yourself altogether.

Aren't you glad Jesus is no respecter of persons?

> For all have sinned and come short of God's glory.
>
> Romans 3:23

> The Lord is not slow about His promise, as some count slowness, but is patient toward you, not wishing for any to perish but for all to come to repentance.
>
> 2 Peter 3:9

Pharmakia

I don't remember his name, but I will never forget his face. If I live to be one hundred, even five hundred, I will not forget. That is all I have ever seen of this young man, his face—actually, just a picture of his face. It was grainy, black and white, and on the front page of the *Los Angeles Times*. It captured a human being's last few seconds of conscious existence.

The photograph framed a man on his hands and knees crawling out of a pool at the Melbourne Zoo in Australia. His face was turned towards the camera but his eyes were turned upward, trying to glimpse the massive polar bear in whose jaws his head was firmly fixed. The eyes were so sad and revealed a mixture of terror, confusion, surprise, and pain. The corners of his mouth were turned down the way they might be just before a huge sob. How could this happen? And why would anybody want to capture this moment of horror on film?

It made an extra large impression on me because, at the time the picture was taken, I was taking care of our zoo's polar bear, Ivan. Ivan was a likely mankiller, and I had suffered many dreams in which I was the man in the photograph. Polar bears are one of the few animals that will hunt man as prey on a normal basis. They may be the animal most feared by zoo personnel in general.

The article explained. It seems the man had taken a rather large dose of LSD. His friend explained that he had hoped that it would help him experience the animals at the zoo at a different level of consciousness. While gazing at the polar bears, he perceived that they wanted to be his friends. Before anyone could stop him, he dove into their pool and swam to greet them. The polar bears greeted him as any predator would greet its prey. The male polar bear was probably slightly confused. Making a kill was not usually this easy, and prey had never offered itself to be killed.

I wondered about the photograph as I examined it for a clue. Was the man's expression the sudden fleeting reflection of one who was aware that he had been lied to? Did he manage one last tragic look at the real world, the world from which he was trying to escape when he began his journey with mind-altering drugs?

This incident was not the only one of its kind. Something very much like it happened at the Los Angeles Zoo several years later. It happened, as far as anyone could tell, late on a weekday afternoon. No one saw it happen, but the evidence told the story so clearly that it read like a book.

The event announced itself suddenly, without warning. The time had come to close the zoo. It was fifteen minutes to five and time to let the animals in for the night. All over the zoo animals were anxiously awaiting the opportunity to receive the best portion of their food and sleep in their comfortable night quarters. Dave, the keeper who cared for the lions, had performed this ritual a thousand times before. The lions' night cages were clean and dry and several pounds of Zupreem Feline Diet were awaiting them. Dave gave a pull on the lever that lifted the guillotine door. It locked into position but no lions ran into the night cage. He looked into the opening created by the raised door and his heart stopped beating. There in the dim light was the female lioness. Her muzzle was bloody and she was snarling over her prey—a man, or what was left of a man. Dave gasped and ran for a phone.

When the investigation was concluded, the man's story was pieced together. This man had chosen phencyclidine hydrochloride to find another less painful plane of existence. Because this drug has so many different effects, it was impossible to determine what motive caused him to take a detour into a nightmare. No note, no friend, no clue as to why this man confronted our lioness in her territory. We were told that he had entered the exhibit by leaping to a palm tree that grew near the twenty-foot wall around the moated area. His arm must have shown the abrasions or his clothes must have disclosed fibers from the tree because the police were certain that this was the way he entered the exhibit.

There was no way of knowing just how the next moments passed. I don't want to know. His death may have been mercifully quick, for no human came forward who had heard him cry out. He must have been sadly alone, with no one present who cared. One of the mysteries was that he was carrying a Bible. No one knew why; no one knew what he was there for.

One of our keepers lost his fingers to a hyena named Hatari. Hatari had been used in the John Wayne movie of the same name. This keeper, while under the influence of marijuana, lost two important qualities necessary for working around wild animals. He lost his good judgment and his timing. While trying to do his job after a brief encounter with a marijuana joint, he stumbled and grabbed for the chain link fence to keep from falling. Hatari was only too glad to take his fingers.

Drugs, more properly called pharmaceuticals, derive their name from the Greek word pharmakia. Whenever this word is translated in the Bible it is rendered sorcery. It was understood to be the devil's work. And so it has become in our age. It's just like the devil to take a wonderful life-saving science like pharmacology and turn it into the number one killer of our youth. Suicide by overdose claims more of our youth than any other single cause of death. In the Book of John, verse 44 of chapter 8, we read about Satan's method of operation. It tells us that Satan is a liar and a murderer and he has been so from the beginning.

Whenever I remember these stories I think of them as prime victories for the enemy. I am as sure as I can be that drug abuse is our nation's number one problem. It is tearing our youth to pieces.

> Be sober, be watchful. Your adversary the devil prowls around like a roaring lion, seeking someone to devour. Resist him, firm in your faith…
>
> 1 Peter 5:8–9

Mrs. Bedlam

The keepers at the Los Angeles Zoo had a saying: "The zoo would be a great place to work if you could just keep the people out." Like any saying, it had a background. Allow me to illustrate.

You would think you could trust senior citizens to behave themselves at the zoo. They were normally our most cherished visitors. But one little old lady engineered a mission of mercy that created more bedlam than any single visitor in the zoo's history. She looked innocent enough. She wore a faded black dress under her full-length black wool coat, and she displayed a wide-brimmed black hat with a silk rose that looked like it had been run over by a bus. But somehow, she passed security and the ticket-takers with two shopping bags filled to the brim with rubber balls. They were all shapes, colors, sizes, and textures.

She had been to the zoo many times before and had concluded the animals were bored. In her mind, she was carrying two bags of recreation.

She threw a ball into the sea lion pool, and I'm sure she felt affirmed as the most playful animal of the zoo pushed it back and forth. She threw them into the bear moats, and the bears ate them, as did the monkeys. We knew that because rubber showed up undigested in their waste material. Many of the animals simply ignored them, but not our female black-maned lioness. The ball thrown into her moated area was made of a very hard, dark blue rubber. The lioness bit down on it so hard that it was impaled on her awesome right canine. No amount of clawing at the ball dislodged it, and the female became increasingly distressed. She rubbed her face on the ground hoping to drag it loose. Her muzzle began to drip blood and mud, and she was salivating profusely. The keeper knew his animal needed help, and he called the health center and begged us to come quickly. The lioness was in trouble.

Dr. Bradford was the veterinarian on duty. He was brand new—just out of school. He had never worked with a lion before. Upon arriving we noticed the keeper had managed to lock the lioness in her night quarters. Dr. Bradford leaned on the bars to get a better look at her problem. She hated people and never tolerated anyone touching her cage. Knowing this, I reached out to pull him away, but it was too late. She lunged at his face and roared. Now a roar under any circumstance is impressive; but inside a small, concrete building, it is a major event. It rumbled through our bodies like thunder and we found ourselves momentarily paralyzed—and we were expecting it. Our young veterinarian wasn't expecting it, so he fainted. He lay on the cement floor for a few seconds. When he had again become coherent, he said something I will not quote in case children are reading this. The essence of his comment was that he now believed in lions.

I think he enjoyed shooting the lioness with the tranquilizer gun and would have enjoyed shooting the little old lady more, but we never saw her again. She did call the next day, though, to see if the animals enjoyed the rubber balls. When she was told how we had to remove the rubber ball with a hacksaw, she hung up.

I think we all understood that her motives were pure, but she clearly demonstrated a human potential. She did the wrong thing for the right reason. She was sincere. But she was sincerely wrong. The effect was the same as doing the wrong thing for the wrong reason. She could not have caused any more trouble if she had intended to harm the lioness.

Her major problem was that she was acting beyond her sphere of authority. She had no permission to act at all. She took this matter into her own hands.

This is when we create the most problems for ourselves—when we take matters into our own hands and act outside of God's authority. Intentions don't cut it. You've heard the old cliché, "The road to hell is paved with good intentions."

Dietrich Bonhoeffer, in his book *Ethics*, makes an interesting observation: "The tree of knowledge of Good and Evil produced the ability to choose our own good or our own evil." Both choices may take us an equal distance from God. But we have a third alternative—God's will.

One of my favorite films is *The Sound of Music*. My favorite moment in the film is when Mother Superior asks Maria, "What is the most important thing you have learned at the abbey?" Maria humbly answers, "To find God's will and do it." God has given us His Word for a lamp to light the way. His will is not hidden. And His Scripture provides all the authority we need to act rightly.

David wrote, "I have laid up Thy word in my heart, that I might not sin against Thee" (Ps. 119:11). He learned to do that after feeling the full effects of taking matters into his own hands.

Stop and think about your life. Do you have permission to be living the way you are? If you are not sure, find out. If you don't, stop whatever you are doing right now...before you get hurt or you hurt someone else.

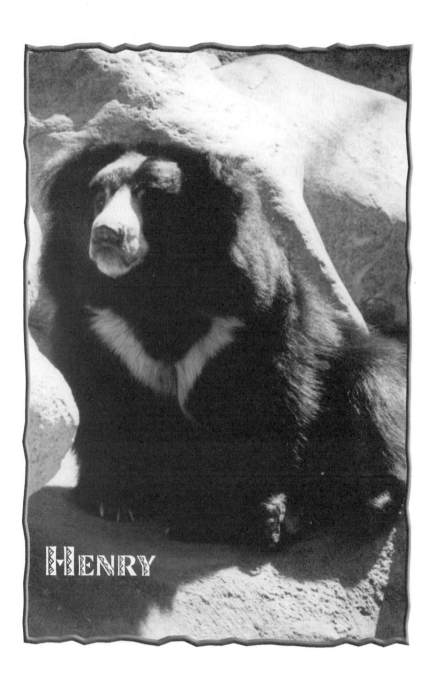

HENRY

Keeping Your Head Above Water

Henry was a sloth bear. Now describing a sloth bear is no simple task, but if you can imagine a bear made out of assorted spare bear parts, you might start to get the picture. Sloth bears are on the small side, weighing not more than 200 pounds. They are bushy all over, particularly around the head. When you look at a sloth bear, you might feel reluctant to ascribe its origin to one of the six days of Creation. Once you've seen one, you might think that way back at the beginning of time a black male lion had married a small female bear. (Maybe the lion had very poor eyesight and the she-bear never bothered to mention that she was a bear.) As a matter of fact, sloth bears look more like something that happened to a bear.

Sloth bears are mostly black, with just a touch of white or gray around their muzzles, but that mostly depends on their age. Tufts of hair stuck up from the ends of their saggy ears. And they are pigeon-toed; they rock back and forth when they walk.

Henry was a prime specimen of sloth bear, but he was also a little more than that. Henry's behavior was as bizarre as bears get. He had several quirks that made him memorable. To give you some idea of how special Henry was, consider this. The zoo owned sixteen bears that represented six different species, but only two were named: Ivan, the 950-pound polar bear, and little Henry, the eccentric sloth bear. Henry threw tantrums. He threw them all the time, and he didn't require much of a reason. Flies buzzing around his head might set him off. Being denied a treat after he had begged for food might do it. Being let in for dinner two minutes late was a sure bet.

You know the expression, "You're acting like a real bear"? The first time they used it, they put Henry's picture next to it—not a full body shot but a close-up of his face. It made you wonder why they named him Henry, unless he was named for Henry VIII. I would have chosen the name Grumpy.

As grouchy as Henry was, you couldn't help but like the little fellow, because he was possessed of the same mettle as Snow White's Grumpy. I saw him as stout-hearted and brave, and it hurts to tell you his story.

Henry had a lot of bad days; he liked it that way. But he liked making them bad himself. One dreary January day, after it had rained for several days, Henry spent the worst day of his life.

Henry's bear moat was constructed below the level of the surrounding drainage system. When water ran into the moat or the surrounding drains they would begin to fill until a float activated a pump that would drain the excess water away. The drains had always worked faithfully, and it never occurred to anyone that one night they would not. The ground was fully saturated and the torrents of water were cascading from the adjacent hillsides as the rain challenged the hillsides with relentless fury.

The pumps had worked overtime for several days in a row, and their strength was failing. Their time was silently at hand. That night as Henry's keeper George left to go home, he could not foresee the nightmare he would face the next morning. He smiled at Henry, who had just come off exhibit and was busy sifting through a pile of delicacies that George had lovingly prepared minutes before. Henry didn't look up when George said good night. It wasn't his way. But this was always the one moment each day when Henry was incapable of hiding his capacity for joy. He loved food, and he didn't care who knew it. The last sounds George heard as he closed the back door of the bear grotto were Henry's ecstatic utterances, spontaneously generated while eating his favorite foods.

When George left, Henry ate and ate until his floor was completely free from any small bit of food. He then licked his paws clean and circled his grotto until he was ready to lie down for the night. Sleep came quickly to a mind with no cares. In no time, Henry was snoring and dreaming of more treats and faraway Eastern jungles with exotic vines and flowers.

Henry was completely unaware that the pump had broken and that the water in his moat was rising at an alarming rate. He did not realize that before morning his grotto could be his tomb. He was surrounded by concrete and steel, and there was no way of escape.

It wasn't until three o'clock in the morning that Henry was awakened by water that was licking at his right paw, which was dangling from his sleeping platform. He stood and viewed something he was still unable to understand. His cage was filling with water. By 3:30 that morning the water had risen to his belly. Nobody was there to see it, but I'm sure Henry threw a tantrum—a first-class tizzy. He probably began by jumping up and down on his front feet. Then in full bad humor, he jumped up and down on all fours. I didn't do any good though, because the water kept rising and was now up to his neck. I believe his instincts to survive were now stimulated and he would have paced with his head high. Minutes later Henry was beyond pacing. He was forced to do what all bears can do so well, stand up. All bears can do it but never have

93

to do it for very long; it just isn't comfortable. Comfort was no longer an option. It was stand or die and the water was still rising.

The only light in the bear grotto was a 25-watt bulb mounted near the ceiling. It case an eerie light that danced dimly across the water to Henry. Henry looked at the back door, which was now four feet deep in water, and wished that George would come through and let him out on exhibit where he could crawl to higher ground. It was now 4:30 in the morning and it would be nearly four hours before keepers began to arrive at the zoo to check on their animals. Henry didn't have that much time. The water was now up to his mouth, and he was standing on his tiptoes to breathe. He still watched the door for George's appearance and moaned sadly because he was afraid. Being a tropical bear, he was not enjoying the cold water that engulfed him. Minutes must have seemed like hours to this frightened little sloth bear. The water had risen even more, and Henry was dancing to keep his head above water. The rain kept coming, and there was no evidence it would stop. The gully where Henry lived looked like a small lake, even outside the grotto. Security knew the tunnel leading to Henry's area was filling up with water, but it did not occur to them that the bear moat was filling up also. No emergency plan was put into action; security thought that maintenance could deal with a plugged drain tomorrow.

When George arrived at the zoo the next morning, he frowned at the perilous gray sky and pulled his rain gear closer to his body as he got out of his car. The rain was coming down harder than ever and stung his face and hands as he walked toward his section. He stopped to chat with Bob Morris, the aquatics keeper, who asked if maybe it was time to start thinking about building an ark. George said he didn't think that was such a far-out idea in light of the number of days in a row that it had rained. They exchanged small talk; then George walked briskly to his section. When he got to the tunnel and saw that it was waist-deep in water, George's heart began to pound. He yelled "HENRY!" and waded through the waist-deep water to the bear moat. A feeling of hopelessness overwhelmed him when he saw the lake that surrounded the bear moat. It was deep, and in George's mind Henry was history. George waded into the icy water and made his way to the back door of the bear's moat. He reached under the water, opened the door, and waded inside. The 25-watt bulb, still working, offered dim light. As George's eyes adjusted, he was able to see something his mind could not comprehend. There were both of Henry's paws reaching as high as they could reach, and more importantly, George could see Henry's nose, about four inches of it, sticking above the water. George was struck silent. And during that silence, he could hear Henry's systematic, rhythmic breathing. It was obvious that he was able to breathe only through his nose. George yelled, "Henry, hang on!" then ran for a telephone.

"Security, call maintenance and tell 'em to bring every pump they have, quickly, or we're going to lose a sloth bear. His moat is filled with water. There isn't a moment to spare. Help me!"

Security got right on it, and soon several maintenance men were busy setting pumps and firing them up. Although he was shivering, George stood chest deep in water to watch his bear. He hoped Henry would survive.

George stared at Henry's nose and thought maybe there was more of it showing. George was shivering violently but declined to leave his bear. He had never felt more helpless in his life. He would love to open Henry's steel door and pull him to safety, but Henry would not have understood. George would have looked like shredded wheat and drowned with him before either of them reached the back door. There are some times one can only wait to see what will happen; this was one of those times.

Henry's feet began to slide slowly down the wall; then suddenly his nose disappeared beneath the water. George's heart began pounding. Had the rescue attempt failed so soon? Ten, fourteen, twenty seconds passed and no Henry. George began to wade toward Henry's door. He had to do something. Thirty seconds, no bear. George fumbled for his keys, and while he did Henry surface, coughing and sputtering. In the darkness of the grotto, Henry had struggled under water to find higher ground. He had mercifully struggled in the right direction. He found the front of the cage where he could stand on his concrete drinker and hold the bars. From this position he would be able to last until the water was drained. Henry shook the water from his face, eyes, and ears, and after he did he found himself staring at George, who was smiling though teary. "Silly old bear," said George as he wiped his nose and choked back a sob.

Henry stared at George—his bear brain trying to sort out whether George was causing this calamity or fixing it. He ended up giving George a what-took-you-so-long look and moaned a little to show his discomfort.

The water was now draining noticeably, and it was clear he would live to throw another tantrum. Hundreds more, maybe thousands. He lived to a ripe old age, impressive for any bear.

How about you? Do your circumstances make you feel like you're struggling just to keep your head above water? Is it dark; and for the life of you, you can't see an end to the trial? This is the time to dig in, hang in, and wait for a chance to get to higher ground.

We are all characters in a book, and maybe the chapter you're in right now isn't going very well at all. I can assure you of two good things: This chapter will end for good or for evil and a better chapter will follow. The really good news is that our book has a happy ending if we know Jesus. If you're the kind that turns to the other end of the book to see how the story ends, then think on these:

> But the people who trust the Lord will become strong again.
>
> Isaiah 40:31

> You will be sad, but your sadness will become joy.
>
> John 16:20

> The only temptations that you have are temptations that all people have. But you can trust God. He will not let you be tempted more than you can stand. But when you are tempted, God will also give you a way to escape that temptation. Then you will be able to stand it.
>
> 1 Corinthians 10:13

> Even when we were with you, we told you that we all would have to suffer.
>
> 1 Thessalonians 3:4

> Share in the troubles that we have. Accept them like a true soldier of Christ Jesus.
>
> 2 Timothy 2:3

Struggling to keep your head above water? Remember…help is on the way. God may seem slow, but He is never late!

Perpetual Adolescents

There are two kinds of chimpanzees: those that let things happen and those that make things happen. Our zoo had both, and they both caused a pile of trouble.

Zoo chimps are bored. They really don't have enough to do and it makes them a little crazy most of the time.

Most of their time is spent waiting. They wait to be let out in the morning. They wait for enough food to get them through the day. They wait to be let in at night so that they can eat their fill and sleep till morning. They watch people watching them and sometimes they throw things at them (disgusting things). They fight a little and play a little, but mostly they wait.

So it's not surprising that the day they were offered an opportunity for diversion they took it. You see, one of the zoo patrons noticed that there was a fifty-foot long, one-inch hose neatly coiled right in front of the chimp exhibit. He must have said to himself, "Self, if you throw that hose over the edge of the exhibit, it will provide an excellent escape ladder for the chimps." And that is exactly what he did.

He couldn't have realized the dangerous situation that he was creating for the public. Most of our chimps were very neurotic, and when they were out of the exhibit they could become quite excited. The adults were four to six times as strong as a man, and a good number of them had periods during which they were very aggressive for no apparent reason.

While the chimps were making their escape, I was counting the minutes until quitting time. That was not my usual practice, but then this was not a usual day. It was June 19th and it was my seventh wedding anniversary. My wife, Carol, would be looking good and my mouth was watering for prime rib. When the phone rang, I felt a twinge of fear that something was going to make me late for our celebration.

I couldn't have been more accurate. A security guard calmly informed us that eight chimpanzees were out of their moated area and mingling with the public. We grabbed our capture equipment and headed out.

When we arrived we were treated to the most frightening sight I have ever witnessed. Jeanie, a highly unpredictable and sometimes very aggressive female, was hovering over a baby stroller. Her mouth was wide open and her lethal teeth were resting against the skull of a three-month-old baby girl. Jeanie was not showing any signs of aggression, but that didn't mean that two seconds later she wouldn't be. The baby's mother looked concerned, but she didn't appear to be unduly frightened. I cautioned our new vet not to make any moves until Jeanie was clear of the baby. Some of the other chimps noticed me because I was in uniform, and they began to hollar. Jeanie looked around, saw us, and took off running. All of the chimps knew we had a tranquilizer gun, and they began to back away. I called out to the zoo patrons that these chimps were very dangerous and told them to leave the area for their own safety. We wouldn't attempt any capture activity until they were safely out of sight.

When we finally exposed the tranquilizer gun, a very funny

thing happened. Toto, our oldest and largest male, led three of the females back to the hose and climbed back into the exhibit. This group huddled together and patted each other. That's what chimps do to comfort each other when they are very upset.

Other keepers began to arrive, and two of the babies recognized them and crawled into their arms. They had sensed the fear in the parents and were in an emotional turmoil. But they calmed down quickly when the keepers carried them to the back of the exhibit.

Only two rebelled—the erratic Jeanie and the delicate Antoinette, more affectionately know as Annie. They climbed the guardrail and made their way deep into the landscaping between their own moat and the Indian rhino yard. Herman, the Indian rhino, was beside himself with rage. He charged and snorted and even reared up slightly hoping to get a chance to bash a chimp.

The growth between the two exhibits was dense and difficult to penetrate. It was a non-negotiable tangle of wild roses and ivy.

Our job was to get into a position to shoot a tranquilizer dart into Jeanie first in the hopes that Annie would surrender and climb back into the moat. Dr. Bradford felt that since he was paid the most, he should take the risk of shooting the angry chimp. I told him I thought he was right. He carried the rifle over the guardrail and I followed him with the pistol. That would be used for backup if the first shot missed. We spread the wild roses apart and saw our two escapees. They were huddled in the shadows and screamed their disapproval at our presence. Dr. Bradford took careful aim and a blast of air propelled a dart swiftly to the generous hindquarters of the female chimpanzee.

Jeanie reacted instantly, but not the way we had hoped. She charged screaming with anger, her teeth showing from ear to ear.

I knew that as soon as she saw the pistol she would stop and run away, but Dr. Bradford didn't know that, so he made a run for it. He was a big man, and when he turned to run he knocked me flat. The pistol went flying. Dr. Bradford tripped over me and began to fall into the rhino moat. Herman, more enraged than ever, was trying his best to horn the doctor. As Dr. Bradford was falling I had grabbed one leg and was holding on to him for dear life. I was sure Jeanie was going to be biting us any second so I had closed my eyes to concentrate on keeping the vet out of the rhino yard. She must have seen the pistol before it went flying and ceased her charge because we were never bitten.

With great effort, the doctor pulled himself back over the edge of the moat and breathlessly thanked me for grabbing him. We peered back into the undergrowth and saw Jeanie showing the effects of the powerful tranquilizer. As we had hoped, Annie jumped back into the exhibit by herself. And three minutes later Jeanie was asleep for the night.

Chimpanzees are perpetual adolescents, never quite ready to take the responsibility for the freedom they so desperately seem to want. Of all the great apes, they are the most playful and the least dignified. They are child-like. At the time of this writing, Toto is nearly fifty years of age and still totally irresponsible. In fact, from what I could gather, he is worse than ever. But it's okay because Toto is a chimp.

One of the fundamental differences between a man and a chimpanzee is that a man may choose to become responsible. If we are responsible we have opted for maturity. We have grown up. If we are possessed of all our faculties, growing up is what we are supposed to do. It is expected of us, and if we don't, someone, usually our parents, are disappointed and embarrassed.

The apostle Paul was disappointed with the church members

at the city of Corinth. They never grew up. His words express his disappointment.

> But I, brethren, could not address you as spiritual men, but as men of the flesh, as babes in Christ. I fed you with milk, not solid food; for you were not ready for it; and even yet you are not ready, for you are still of the flesh. For while there is jealousy and strife among you, are you not of the flesh, and behaving like ordinary men?
>
> 1 Corinthians 3:1–3

It's not that they didn't have the knowledge that adults acquire, because they did. It's not that they didn't have the Spirit of God, because they did. They were babies because they couldn't take the responsibility for the freedom to serve and obey Christ. They wouldn't care for others. Like children and adolescents they simply focused on their own needs. But the mature in Christ focus on the needs of others.

The author of Hebrews directs his thoughts to the same issue: maturity.

> About this we have much to say which is hard to explain, since you have become dull of hearing. For though by this time you ought to be teachers, you need some one to teach you again the first principles of God's word. You need milk, not solid food; for every one who lives on milk is unskilled in the word of righteousness, for he is a child. But solid food is for the mature, for those who have their faculties trained by practice to distinguish good from evil.
>
> Hebrews 5:11–14

Maturity Test

1. On whose needs are you focused?
2. Are you consistent in doing the right thing?

3. Are you serving others?

If you have been a Christian for some time, I can say something to you I could never say to a chimp. "Don't you think it's time to grow up?" If you haven't been a Christian for some time, then you may need to know that the questions should have been answered like this: 1) Others; 2) Yes; 3) Yes.

Practice what you learn in the faith as you learn it. In no time at all you will be maturing nicely.

It Will Be Different For Me

Bandit was irresistible. No raccoon that ever existed had more natural "cute" than this ninety-day-old bundle of mischief. When my neighbor Julie bought him at the pet store, she was sure they would be lifelong friends. Everywhere she went, he went—usually perched on her shoulder. Bandit's habit of holding Julie's cheeks in his paws and looking into her eyes with sparkling curiosity always melted her and solicited an affectionate kiss and hug. And he grew. Eighteen months passed and Bandit became a strapping twenty-five-pound adolescent raccoon, still full of the dickens and only slightly less playful. He still loved affection, rode on shoulders, and seemed to be a one-raccoon advertisement that raccoons make great pets.

I mentioned Julie and Bandit to our zoo veterinarian one day and inquired as to why more people didn't keep raccoons as pets. His answer floored me. "They undergo a glandular change at about twenty-four months. After that, they become unpredictable, independent, and often attack their owners."

"Are there exceptions?" I inquired.

"None that I know of," he said thoughtfully.

"Then Julie is likely to be bitten?"

"Any time now, I should think," the doctor added with

conviction.

Since a thirty-pound raccoon can be equal to a one-hundred-pound dog in a scrap, I felt compelled to mention the coming change to Julie. She sat and listened politely as I explained what an eminent world authority had shared with me concerning raccoons and their nature. I'll never forget her answer.

"It will be different for me...Bandit is different." And she smiled as she added, "Bandit wouldn't hurt me. He just wouldn't!"

Three months later, Julie underwent plastic surgery for facial lacerations sustained when her adult raccoon attacked her for no apparent reason. Bandit was released into the wild.

That happened years ago, and I've heard Julie's reply many times since: "But it will be different for me."

Rob, a sixteen-year-old boy, said, "I know what I'm doing. It's different for me. I know all about dosages and stuff. My dad is a pharmacist." Rob overdosed six months later and spent two months in a mental ward.

Judy, a fifteen-year-old girl, argued, "I know he's been around, but it's different with us. He really loves me. He really does." Judy is now twenty-five and living at home with her nine-year-old son. The son never met his father.

Jerry, an eighteen-year-old college student, declared, "I'm different. A few drinks don't slow me down a bit." Jerry is dead now, and he took three friends with him when he drove off an embankment. They were all drunk.

Pat, a thirty-five-year-old woman, contended, "My kids are different. They will be able to handle the divorce find. I'll spend more time with them. Besides, my lover is great with kids." Pat divorced her husband and got remarried to her lover. She divorced again after he tried to kill her. The children didn't sleep well for years and needed to see a counselor weekly.

David, a forty-plus-year-old executive, reasoned, "Wow, she's beautiful! Her husband is away on a business trip. Nobody will know. It will be different, exciting, temporary." David ended up causing this man's wife to be pregnant. To avoid scandal, he had the man killed. He felt compelled to marry the woman; then her baby died. David's life was never the same again. That incident caused members of his family to turn against him, and one of his children even tried to kill him. I'm sure he never dreamed that things would get so tangled. I'm sure he thought, "It will be different for me." (You can find this executive's biography beginning in 2 Samuel 11.)

Let's take one step back and look at our lives. Are we in violation of some well-know axiom? Are our closest friends or relatives warning us about something? Are we in conflict with the clear teaching of the Scriptures?

Now, repeat out loud the following phrase, "Maybe it won't be different for me."

CHAMEROUN

ANYBODY FOR
AN ELEPHANT?

You never know what might happen when you do someone a favor. When an admiral of the United States Navy tried to help out the premier of Cambodia, it led to all sorts of trouble for the Los Angeles Zoo.

This is a shameful story. Only the names have been changed, as there is no further need to embarrass any of the irresponsible parties.

During the late 1960s and early 1970s Los Angeles was known to be the only city in the United States with its own foreign policy. Our mayor was out of town as often as possible nursing a delusion of grandeur and embracing thoughts of the presidency. He was always speaking on behalf of our Vietnam policy and making lots of friends in the military. It was one of those friendships that led to the Los Angeles Zoo being asked to accept a male elephant. The story the veterinarians and I received firsthand from the assistant director of the zoo was stranger than fiction.

The premier of Cambodia had become deathly ill and was in need of a delicate surgical process not available in his own country. The nearest help available was on an American aircraft carrier stationed off the coast of his embattled kingdom. So the navy flew him to the carrier and a team of expert surgeons saved his life.

The Cambodians had a strange way of saying thank you. A simple "thank-you" note would have been more than enough, but tradition is tradition and must be observed. The Cambodian tradition demanded that a male elephant be given to the man most responsible for the saving of another's life. And the premier decided that the admiral directing the fleet operations from the aircraft carrier was the man deserving of the honor.

Now the admiral was the epitome of a crusty old salt. He had a raspy voice, short white hair, and skin wrinkled and blotched from thousands of hours of chafing wind, salt spray, and reflected sun from all the seas of the world. He was just the kind of man who didn't need an elephant. But it would be an unforgivable breach of protocol to refuse a gift of such magnitude. So in the style of a man who has learned to survive wars and presidents, he acknowledged the offer and began making plans to accept the elephant. I'll bet you're thinking, "What's the problem? A free elephant sounds like a pretty great deal, right?" Wrong.

The problem is that the elephant was a male. Male elephants are dangerous. They resist training and become unmanageable at various times during the year. After many deaths of keepers and trainers, zoos throughout the world had decided to keep only females.

When the admiral called the mayor we assume the conversation must have proceeded something like this.

"Mayor, it's the admiral. Your city has a fine zoo I'm told."

"Yes, Admiral, I practically built it myself."

"The wife and I have come by a little gift and we would like to donate it to your zoo."

"Sounds great, Admiral. What is it?"

"It's a male elephant, Mayor."

"Sounds like a generous gift. Let me call our people at the zoo and make the arrangements."

So the mayor called the zoo. We know how the conversation went on our end.

"Mayor, we really can't accept the male elephant. It's just too dangerous. That animal would hurt somebody out here. You could count on it, Your Honor. We have no quarters in which to keep it."

The mayor took the news reluctantly and phoned the hopeful admiral to break the bad news. At this point we can only speculate on the pressure that was exerted on the mayor. Anyway, the mayor called back our way and addressed our director in the following manner.

"I would consider it a personal favor if you would provide a home for the admiral's elephant. It will require that you send some of your staff to Cambodia to pick it up. The navy will pick up the tab, and your people will go first class. I trust you'll have everything arranged at the zoo so that we can say thank you for the admiral's generous gift. By the way, the admiral's wife has made a small request. She would like the tusks as a souvenir. I trust you will work that out also. I really do appreciate your cooperation in this opportunity to help our country."

It would be impossible to refuse to do the mayor a personal favor, so our director "Yes, Your Honored" him half to death and agreed to care for a male elephant. He was met with a lot of resistance by the staff, but no one wanted to call the mayor back so a date was fixed. A team was sent to the other side of the earth to receive an expensive gift. Expensive for us, that is. It was to cost America more than three hundred thousand dollars just to accept the elephant.

To tell you the truth, there were a number of us that would have loved to go to Cambodia, and we were disappointed when only one keeper was chosen. The director and the head administrator of the Los Angeles Zoo Association went to handle the protocol and make the necessary arrangements. A crate would need to be built and preparations for the extensive flight would need to be made.

Our clever director had the enormous crate built out of teak he purchased, tons of it, all of which was to become his when the elephant was unloaded at the Los Angeles Zoo.

The group was gone for two weeks, and the zoo was abuzz with gossip and speculation concerning the male elephant. Every keeper was sure that they would have told the mayor where to get off, but theirs was breaktime bravery. We all would have done what the director did. Still, breaktime was the only opportunity we got to direct the zoo, and we tried to make the best of it.

The return was well attended by those who anticipated a raging bull elephant. The crate was a good deal larger than expected. The teak was unfinished and no one suspected that it had any value at all—in reality, it was worth a fortune. When the door was swung open, the keeper who had been flown to Cambodia led the elephant out of the crate.

He was the most pitiful specimen we had ever seen. He was suffering from malnutrition and was clearly depressed. His eyes lacked luster, and even walking was an effort.

We were told that the little male's name was Chameroun (Sham-ah-roon), which means "prosperity" in Cambodian. If this poor excuse for an Asian elephant was their idea of prosperity, we were being given a graphic display of how depleted their nation had become.

As the veterinarian and I began the examination, we discovered one thing after another that would require extensive treatment. Chameroun was filled with internal parasites, which explained his poor condition. He would have to be isolated from the other elephants for weeks while he was being treated. He also had suspicious looking lumps all over his body, which turned out to be another type of worm that burrows under the skin. Each worm would need to be removed surgically. It was a process that would take hours and hours.

Chameroun was too weak to be tranquilized, so the removing of his tusks for the admiral's wife would have to wait until his condition improved dramatically.

As time passed, Chameroun did improve. But as he improved he became less docile. It was clear that it would only be a matter of time until somebody got hurt. No one can stop an angry elephant from doing harm if harm is what it wants to do.

The official day to say thank you to the premier of Cambodia and the admiral came with pomp and pageantry. The zoo director thanked the mayor for the contact that led to the procurement of this rarely exhibited animal. The mayor thanked the admiral and his wife for thinking of Los Angeles when it came time to find a home for the generous gift, and he thanked America for giving him the opportunity to serve his world. Cambodian officials again thanked the admiral for saving their beloved premier.

I never expect to see that many liars plying their trade in one location again. No greater invitation for lightning has ever been issued unanswered.

The best thing that happened that day was a visit by the beautiful actress Candice Bergen. She was there gathering information for an uncomplimentary article that she was writing about the mayor. The article was entitled, "The Man in the Empty Suit." Several keepers were only too glad to explain how the mayor's pressure on the zoo to accept the elephant was sure to lead to the injury or even death of anyone responsible for its care.

The keepers were prophetic. An incident did occur which could have been fatal. A keeper sustained a severe back injury from Chameroun, and plans were made to remove the elephant from the collection. After two years, the now healthy but unpredictable male was donated to a zoo in Mexico, where he lived until the end of his days.

As I thought through this story, I found three lessons that begged to be taught. First, there were many times for people to say no. The admiral could have refused to take the elephant, and in so doing saved the United States government three hundred thousand dollars. The mayor could have refused the admiral's offer when he discovered the danger factor in order to protect the keepers. The director could have said no on general principles and stood by the men that he was responsible to protect. Learning when to say no to situations that have no value or are counterproductive divide wise men from fools. But this story owned no wise men.

Second, we are never bound to obey anybody else's traditions. My boss, Dr. Charles Sedgwick, the greatest zoo veterinarian ever, once told me—and I quote—"Gary, always be loyal to your own principles and you'll never have to worry whom to be loyal to." We only have to listen to the Scripture and our own conscience. Any other voices need not apply.

Third, we need to know that there are unexpected costs when we go out of our way to help others. By saving the premier's life, the admiral chose to be a Good Samaritan.

If we choose to play the roll of the Good Samaritan, and we should, it is sure to cost us more than we will first anticipate. Do you remember the story of the Good Samaritan? It is found in Luke 10:25–37.

And behold, a certain lawyer stood up and put him to the test, saying, "Teacher, what shall I do to inherit eternal life?" And He said to him, "What is written in the Law? How does it read to you?" And he answered and said, "You shall love the Lord your God with all your heart, and with all your soul, and with all your strength, and with all you mind; and your neighbor as yourself." And He said to him, "You have answered correctly; do this, and you will live." But wishing to justify himself, he said to Jesus, "And who is my neighbor?" Jesus replied and said, "A certain man was going down from Jerusalem to Jericho; and he fell among robbers, and they stripped him and beat him, and went off leaving him half dead. And by chance a certain priest was going down that road, and when he saw him, he passed by on the other side. And likewise a Levite also, when he came to the place and saw him, passed by on the other side. But a certain Samaritan, who was on a journey, came upon him; and when he saw him, he felt compassion, and came to him, and bandaged up his wounds, pouring oil and wine on them; and he put him on his own beast, and brought him to an inn, and took care of him. And on the next day to took out two denarii and gave them to the innkeeper and said, 'Take care of him; and whatever more you spend, when I return, I will repay you.' Which of these three do you think proved to be a neighbor to the man who fell into the robbers' hands?" And he said, "The one who showed mercy toward him." And Jesus said to him, "Go and do the same."

The Good Samaritan was good because he went out of his way. He even anticipated that the favor would cost more than he had already paid. It cost him time, energy, and money—and there isn't much more that we can give.

I have a close friend that tells a story of his youth. Sonny was late to school and had chosen to hitchhike to get there quicker. Fortunately, a benevolent old man pulled over and picked him up.

Sonny thanked him for his kindness and they made small talk as they motored down Washington Boulevard in Pasadena. Sonny broke into their conversation and said, "You can let me off here, sir."

The old man looked to both sides of the street and said in a confused tone, "But I don't see any school, son."

"The school's a block up, sir; I can walk. I don't want to take you out of your way."

The old gentleman spoke in a firm but kind way, and said, "Son, when I stopped and picked you up a few minutes ago, I set out to do you a favor. Now if I don't go out of my way, I don't figure I've done you one."

Take a moment and think. When was the last time you went out of your way to do anybody a favor? What did it cost you? If you thought of something recent, thank the Lord. You're becoming more like Jesus. If you couldn't think of anything, don't stand around feeling guilty—go help somebody. Needy folks are all around us.

THE THEME BUILDING

The zoo was opened in September of 1966. It began its marbled history as the world's fifth largest zoo and is the only zoo in modern history that was actually opened as a major zoo. In addition, it had several distinctions. First, we accumulated more rare and endangered animals than any other zoo in the world. And second, by the end of our third year 52 percent of our collections was breeding annually. Those two statistics were very prized in the zoo world and commanded an early respect. But they also engendered a fair amount of jealousy.

There were many criticisms of the Los Angeles Zoo when it was first built. Some were justified and some were not. For starters, it was built on a golf course which had produced a fair amount of revenue for the city, whereas the zoo lost a bundle every year. Also, the newly planted grounds made it look like a desert. During the first summers the zoo sun fried anybody foolish enough to come without some sort of shade, and visitors were blinded by the stark grey exhibits wherever they went. It was often accused of being a concrete jungle. And it was.

The zoo was often criticized for its lack of showmanship as well. The supervisors resented presenting animals in acts of any kind. Their philosophy was that a zoo was an educational institution and ought not to pander to man's baser desires to be entertained when he ought to be educated.

The zoo was divided into nine sections: North America, South America, Africa, Australia, and Eurasia. Then there were the specialty sections: aquatics, birds, reptiles, and the children's petting zoo and nursery. The public rejected this arrangement at first because it made seeing their favorite type of animal more difficult. If you like monkeys for instance, you would have to visit Africa, Eurasia, and South America to see them all, and in so doing you would have seen a number of animals you didn't want to see.

In the middle of the zoo stands its most prominent architectural feature—the Theme Building. It is placed on a rise that overlooks a fair portion of the main zoo, and its twin spires ascend ten stories into the sky. It is African, Indian, and Asian in appearance and really does set the architectural mood for the rest of the zoo. It's called the Theme Building, but what it really turned out to be was an extremely expensive roof with a dirt floor. You see, the committee that worked with the architect could not agree on what should go under the magnificent roof. The architect was able to convince them that they could decide later what should be built underneath it. As for now, he said, it set the theme and was too important to his concept to be left out. And so it was built.

As time passed, the debate raged on. Some thought the Theme Building should be turned into an expensive restaurant, others a gift shop, and some an educational center. Year followed year and all that the roof ever achieved was to provide shade for picnickers. Inexpensive benches were placed there and there under its ample eaves and zoo patrons simply ate lunches they had furnished for themselves.

The zoo has changed in hundreds of ways in the last twenty years. Waterfalls and expensive rock works are everywhere. The trees are tall and full and provide more than enough shade for the zoo patrons at any hour of the day. The animal collection is rare and beautiful, and not many people are complaining anymore. It is really a beautiful zoo, one of the very best. But you know what? The finest architectural monument at the zoo is still a million-dollar roof with a dirt floor. It stands empty after all these years. The biggest change to occur to the building was when the spires had to be sawed off because they had become termite-infested and weak. All because no decision could be made about what should go inside it.

When I think about the Theme Building, it makes me wonder how many people go for twenty or thirty or seventy years without bringing something meaningful into their lives. The prophet Elijah spoke to his own people who could not decide who to bring into their lives. His speech may be found in 1 Kings 18:21:

> And Elijah came near to all the people, and said, "How long will you go limping with two different opinions? If the LORD is God follow him; but if Baal, then follow him." And the people did not answer a word.

We were designed to be God's architectural wonder. We were made to be the temple of the Holy Spirit. Are you standing empty without His presence? Are you existing without anything inside? If you haven't before—let Him build your life into something meaningful.

SALLY

What's It To You?

There was no doubt in my mind that my wife, Carol, was interested when I confessed that I was finding myself attracted to a twenty-four-year-old redhead named Sally. I shared that Sally was short, had beautiful brown eyes, was extremely affectionate, and was absolutely brilliant. I told her how Sally's auburn-red hair trailed gently down her back, arms, legs and feet, and she even had some on her head. Carol was entertained when I admitted that Sally was an orangutan. Sally was under my care at the zoo's health center while her assigned mate, Eli, was being treated for tuberculosis in an adjacent cage.

Sally and Eli were as different as night and day. Sally was a butterball, sweet, helpful, gentle, and smart as a whip. Eli was grouchy, calculating, meaner than sin, and stronger than an ox.

Let me tell you some stories that will help you to know them better. Sally will always be my favorite animal; I will begin with her.

Any keepers worth their salt will offer their great apes something to do. In the wild these animals spend their time looking for food and shelter. Since those things are provided in a zoo, there is nothing for these intelligent and sensitive apes to do but watch an endless stream of people watching them. If you could imagine watching a movie which had no change of scenery, an ever changing cast, and no plot, then you have conceived what a great ape's existence might be like without a creative keeper. Lack of occupation leads to abnormal and aggressive behavior.

I loved to give Sally things to do because she always participated so enthusiastically. Problem-solving was her forte. So I gave her lots to solve.

I would line up twenty peanuts exactly three feet out from the bars of her cage and give her a bath towel. Then Sally would fish for the peanuts by repeatedly casting the towel over them. Little by little she would drag them one at a time to the cage and place them in a neat little pile. She was so decent and orderly that I'm sure she was a Presbyterian.

I'll never forget the day of Sally's great discovery. I set up the peanuts in the normal fashion and handed her a white bath towel. She carefully unfolded it and draped it over her considerable lap, studying it thoughtfully. Then she gave me that "Eureka!" look. She got up quickly and scooted to her drinker, dragging the towel behind her. She looked back at me, and her expression told me she was onto something big. She dipped the towel in and out of the drinker several times until she was satisfied that is was thoroughly soaked. Then she wrung out the excess water. She ambled over to where I had placed the twenty peanuts and cast her wet towel over five of them. She retrieved them with just one effort. I was astounded. To tell you the truth, I'm not sure that I would have reasoned that a wet towel would have increased my advantage. But Sally did. Sally viewed food as her great necessity. And you know what they say, "Necessity is the mother of invention."

Sally's love for food bordered on lust, and she developed whole routines to gain our empathy and attention. She would begin with lip-smacking and graduate to body-slapping. When we looked at her she would smile a gargantuan smile and point to her mouth. If nothing else worked she would croak forth with grunts and barking sounds that clearly displayed her frustration. One day she took a more direct approach.

I was passing by her cage to deliver a bunch of grapes to some primates at the back of the health center. Suddenly, Sally's mighty hand shot through the bars and grasped my arm with her iron grip. She gently but firmly pulled me close to the bars and pointed to the grapes. She smiled. There was no doubt in my mind that she wanted the grapes, and I found that a perfectly convenient time to let her have them. She took them in a most ladylike manner and delicately laid them on her sleeping bench. Keeping my arm firmly in her grasp, she reached out for the hand which had held the grapes, drew it slowly to her mouth, and kissed it. Then she patted me on the back as if to say, "Keep up the good work."

Sally was also helpful. She delighted in scraping up her leftover food into a neat pile and dropping it just outside her cage. On one morning I filled a bucket with warm soapy water and set it right next to her cage. I showed her how to clean the bars of her cage using a bath towel and then gave her the bath towel. She worked diligently for forty minutes scrubbing, rinsing, and wringing. She cleaned all the bars, her sleeping bench, and her holding cage. That little effort won her a vanilla malt.

When Sally was finally allowed to be caged with Eli she became a prolific breeder. She is the mother of at least seven offspring. But her first birth was the most dramatic. Her baby Jonathan was born still encased in the placental sack. She had no idea that she needed to remove it, and we all watched in terror as she sat doing nothing while her newborn was dying for lack of oxygen. Finally, Dr. Sedgwick rushed in, at some personal risk, and took the baby. Nearly five minutes had passed before he tore the

tiny orangutan from its birthing sack. The baby was cool, still, and
hadn't taken a breath. He began CPR and stimulated the body
with deliberate massage. Still no breathing or heartbeat. Dale
Thompson, the keeper who was assisting Dr. Sedgwick, asked,
"What do we do now?"

He heroic vet looked up long enough to say, "We don't give up.
We never give up."

He injected a heart stimulant and the baby stiffened in
response. All present cheered and then held their breath to see
what would come of the doctor's last chance to retrieve the baby's
ebbing life. The heartbeat was weak at first, and then it began to
increase in volume and regularity. Jonathan would live. He will
always be a little slow because of the severe oxygen deficit he
suffered at birth, but he is alive and well and is bringing a great
deal of pleasure to thousands of zoo visitors. Sally had allowed the
doctor to help.

Sally is really something. Visitors to the Los Angeles Zoo still
watch her perform her hilarious food routines. She has added a
new gesture that I had never noticed while she was under my care.
She uses her hand to shade her eyes from the glare of the sun.

Eli was nothing like Sally. He spent every waking moment
looking for opportunities to pull keepers through the bars of his
cage. We had to be watchful while walking near his cage because
he had the kind of strength necessary to tear a man's arm off. A San
Francisco zookeeper lost his arm to a large male orangutan during
a careless moment.

I once saw Eli perform a feat of strength that made me a
believer. Eli's cage was positioned next to a garage door that was
opened every morning to ventilate the health center. When the
door was opened the spring was extended precariously close to Eli's
cage. Eli was able to twang the spring with his longest massive

finger. No matter where I worked in the health center I could hear the monotonous twang as he plucked at it with regularity.

In the back of my mind, I knew that someday he would grasp the spring with his whole hand. I did not think I would actually see it happen, but I did. Eli was in late adolescence and was growing rapidly toward adulthood.

I was heading back to the orangutans' area after checking on the other animals under my care at the center. When I rounded the corner, I stopped in amazement. Eli had a full grasp of the spring and was pulling it into his cage. He resembled a giant hairy Robin Hood pulling a long bow to its limit. The whole garage door assembly bent towards the cage, and then he grabbed that. He pulled with all his might and ended up pulling bolts through a cracking and splintering four-by-four. By the time we were able to remove the assembly, he had tied the metal spring into several knots.

After I witnessed that incident, I added a foot or two onto the already respectful distance that I walked from his cage. And there were more incidents to follow.

Eli delighted in breaking things. One day he managed to stuff his whole body underneath his sleeping bench. The sleeping bench was welded securely to the bars of his cage about eighteen inches off the floor. Eli flexed every muscle in his powerful body. The two-inch by six-inch boards that were bolted to the sleeping bench cracked, then shattered all over the floor of his cage. Eli chose the largest board and fashioned it into a lever. He jammed the lever between the chain that secured the door and the bars of his cage. He pulled with all of his strength but succeeded only in breaking the lever. We were glad.

The most frightening incident occurred at feeding time at the health center. It was ten o'clock in the morning. The vet and I were just finishing our lunch. A bloodcurdling, bone-chilling scream exploded the morning stillness and we looked at each other, both knowing what was happening. Ken, the keeper in the cage room, was in Eli's grasp. If we didn't get there quickly, Ken's chances of survival were slim to none. We leaped out of our chairs and headed for the cage room with reckless abandon. I veered off to grab the capture gun that always intimidated Eli. He wouldn't know if it were loaded or not. The doctor unlocked the cage room door and we burst through the opening together. Ken was screaming at the top of his lungs and we were hoping that we were not too late to save a hand or fingers. As we rounded the corner we saw that other help had arrived before us. Ken's senior keeper was poised to swing a shovel at Eli's hand. Ken had managed to turn his arm so that Eli could not pull it through the bars. Eli was trying his best to turn his arm while the senior keeper was trying to get a line on hitting Eli's hand with the shovel. The senior took a powerful swing. This was no time to hold back. Eli was mean but he wasn't stupid, and he removed his hand at the last possible second. The shovel connected with Ken's arm, causing him much more injury than Eli had.

Ken was knocked backwards a safe distance from the cage. He looked up at the senior keeper and said, "Bill, whose side are you on anyway?"

Eli wouldn't let you like him. Because of his meanness I gave him satisfactory, but not exceptional, care. There were many times that Sally procured treats that I denied Eli. I didn't mind cleaning up after Sally when I had given her a magazine to look at, but I did Eli. The bottom line was Sally was easy to love but Eli wasn't. I really had to force myself to be nice to him.

As time passed I learned the difference between the good keepers and the great. The great simply gave their best to all their animals whether their animals performed or not.

I'm sure that this is what God expects from Christians. Jesus shares a verse that haunts me when I try to apply it to my life. It may be found in Luke 6:27–36. See how it affects you:

> But I say to you that hear, love your enemies, do good to those who hate you, bless those who curse you, pray for those who abuse you. To him who strikes you on the cheek, offer the other also; and to him that takes away your coat do not withhold even your shirt. Give to everyone who begs from you; and of him who takes away your goods do not ask them again.
>
> And as you wish that men would do to you, do so to them. If you love those who love you, what credit is that to you? For even sinners love those that love them. And if you do good to those who do good to you, what credit is that to you? For even sinners do the same. And if you lend to those from whom you hope to receive, what credit is that to you? Even sinners lend to sinners, to receive as much again. But love your enemies, and do good, and lend, expecting nothing in return; and your reward will be great, and you will be sons of the Most High; for He is kind to the ungrateful and the selfish. Be merciful even as your Father is merciful.

Think it over.

ELI

Enter The Villain

It was early in the winter of 1968 when I was sent to the Los Angeles Zoo's version of Siberia. I had participated in the development of our local chapter of the American Association of Zoo Keepers, and most of our keepers were becoming involved in the organization. It was merely an educational fellowship, but our acting director was sure that it would become a labor union. He did everything he could to discourage our growth, and he even made attempts to control our activities. The group met after hours, off of zoo property, and we paid for our own speakers out of our own pockets.

One afternoon the director invited me to his office and told me what the organization could and could not print in our monthly newsletter. I was our group's vice president in charge of programming, and I made it clear that what we did on our own time with our own money was our concern and our concern only. I was insulted, and I told him that he had no more right directing our activities than those of the Boy Scouts of America. Our meeting came to an abrupt halt, and I was excused.

Two weeks later my supervisor came to me and said, "Richmond, I have bad news for you. You've been transferred to the 410 section."

The 410 section was reserved for those to be punished. It was larger than any section in the zoo and contained more animals than could be cared for in eight hours of work. I was sick for two reasons. One, I had known other keepers whose spirits had been broken by the immensity of the task. They were good men who had been drained of joy and heart. And two, I was very happy where I was.

I worked with Dr. Charles Sedgwick, the zoo's beloved veterinarian, caring for the animals at the health center. He was a thoughtful and considerate supervisor and was more than willing to spend every spare moment answering my endless string of questions. That time was the highlight of my zoo career. But it was now being ended by a man that I thoroughly disliked and had now begun to loathe.

I asked why I was being transferred, and the answer I was given was, "The acting director believes you have real potential and said it was time to broaden your horizons."

I was trained for two days on the 410 section, then I was left on my own. It didn't take me long to discover that I could not do the work in eight hours; it would take at least ten. I came in an hour early each morning and I stayed an hour later each afternoon and worked through my break times so that I might have a nice-looking section. I even at my lunch on the run, vowing that the acting director would not break my spirit. The energy that motivated me was the hatred that was growing in my soul. The section became a showcase, and I received satisfaction from the thought that the man might be bothered because I was doing the job. I was beating Siberia.

Then the rains came. It was the only year of my life that it rained for eighteen consecutive days in Southern California. I had to move tons of dirt that had washed to the bottom of my exhibits back to the top. That was when my spirit began to die. The man who had done this to me would often drive by my section in his green Dodge Dart. I would gnash my teeth and get so angry that I would get an upset stomach. I entertained fantasies of the man dying in a fiery car crash. I even hoped the zoo's king cobra would bite him since I knew he could never survive. I hated him. I never thought about it. I just did.

It never occurred to me how my life was looking to others. I felt justified in my hatred. But I was to find out how I looked— the hard way.

My senior keeper's name was Scott. He confided in me one day that he was discouraged with life. He was drinking more than he thought he should, he was depressed, he didn't feel any sense of purpose in life, and he was losing his family. I thought this a perfect time to share my faith in Christ.

"Have you ever though about turning your life over to Christ?" I said in my most thoughtful and caring voice.

"Yeah," he said, "But I decided not to."

"Why?" I probed.

"Because all Christians are hypocrites."

"I'm a Christian and I'm not a hypocrite."

He smiled and said, "You are too." It was a disconcerting smile.

"Why do you say that?" I asked, hoping he didn't have a good reason.

"Aren't Christians supposed to love their enemies?"

"Yes."

"You hate the director's guts. I've seen you look at him like you want to kill him, and you bad-mouth him all the time. I'd say that is hypocrisy."

I was stunned. Everything he said was true. I sat there quietly for a moment trying to think of something clever to say, but nothing clever came. So I said, "You're right. I'm sorry I've been such a crummy example."

"You and everybody else," he said as he walked off.

I'm not sure that I have ever felt as ashamed as I did during that conversation. I asked the Lord's forgiveness and asked him to free me from the terrible hatred that had consumed my thoughts and directed my life. He did, because as 1 John 1:9 promises, "If we confess our sins, he is faithful and just, and will forgive our sins and cleanse us from all unrighteousness."

I was transferred from the 410 section a few weeks later when tears in the muscles of my lower abdomen made performing the task impossible. Eventually, I was transferred back to the health center and promoted to the same position that I was removed from several months before—you guessed it, by the acting director, the man who had punished me. We became friends.

> Being confident of this very thing, that He who has begun a good work in you will perform it unto the day of Jesus Christ.
>
> Philippians 1:6

BLACK WIDOW SAFARI

The greatest lesson I have learned from the animals was not learned at the zoo. It was learned in a mossy, moldy greenhouse in the backyard of a lady I was sure was a witch.

Spring was just giving way to summer. School was almost out, and like all eight-year-old boys I was looking forward to three months of no shoes, except on Sunday, and a creative string of adventures yet to be lived out. My mother was just beginning to fix dinner when the afternoon stillness was broken by the persistent ring of the front doorbell. At the door stood an older man. His tie was loosened and he was drenched with perspiration. He wiped the sweat from his forehead and began his to-the-point presentation, one that he had probably given fifty times before coming to our front door.

"Hello, Ma'am. My name is Edgar Beasly and I'm from the health department. We are going door-to-door to alert people to the fact that they need to spray for black widow spiders. I bet you have already noticed that there are more spiders than usual. Doctors are reporting many bites that they feel are probably black widow bites. Last week a little girl nearly died from one. So we're here to warn you that we are having an epidemic of black widow spiders in Alta Dena, California. This sometimes happens after a real wet spring."

He handed my mother a little book and said, "Ma'am, here's a pamphlet that gives you some real important information about black widows. It shows you what they look like and more importantly what their webs look like. We'd sure be much obliged if you'd spray."

When Mr. Beasly left, my mother scanned the pamphlet. She stared at me with legitimate concern and said, "Gary, if I every catch you so much as walking by a black widow spider web, I'll spank your back-side shiny. Do you understand me, young man?"

I nodded that I did and she handed me the pamphlet. I was fascinated. On the cover was a menacing picture of a female black widow. She looked large and was posed so that she revealed the red hourglass on the underside of her shiny black abdomen. The pamphlet made note that she lived in an irregular web that would likely be found in dark places like garages, wood piles, and under cabinets.

The section that most caught my interest was entitled, "The Bite of the Black Widow Spider." It said that a person who was bitten might experience the following symptoms: discoloration at the site of the bite, nausea, a severe headache, unusual swelling, labored breathing, and blurred vision. It concluded that some children even died from the bite of the black widow spider.

My mother never realized that she had just provided a road map for my next great adventure: the black widow safari. I couldn't wait to tell my best friend, Doug, about the greatest idea of my life.

"Now here it is, Doug. On Saturday morning my parents will be gone for three hours. I figure that will give us time to catch ten black widow spiders. We can take those bandits down to Eliot Junior High School and dump them on this red ant hill that I found. It will be great. The red ants will come streaming out to protect their home and there will be a scary fight. The red ants will win and we will have done our part in Altadena's battle to fight the black widows."

"What if we get bit?" Doug asked.

"We're not going to let those child-killers get us. We'll be real careful. Hey, you're not going to chicken out on me, are you?"

"Well, no," Doug added defensively.

I made Doug perform the bloodbrother handshake and promise not to tell any living soul what we were going to do at 8:30 Saturday morning. He took the oath, knowing that if he broke it his teeth and hair would fall out. I found an old peanut butter jar and poked a few holes in its lid. We didn't want any of the spiders dying before they got a chance to fight the red ants. We chose a two-foot stick for catching the spiders, and then we hid our safari gear behind the garage until Saturday.

As soon as my parents left to go shopping, I ran to Doug's house. He was already waiting for me in his front yard. We grabbed our gear and headed for my backyard. I had already located several webs. On the way there we ran into another good friend, Eric, who was coming over to see if we could play. We finally decided that we'd better let him in, but we made him take an even more solemn oath than Doug had taken.

"What kind of oath?" asked Eric.

"The kind that if you break it something scary happens."

Eric really wanted in so he took the oath.

"I, Eric…"

"I, Eric…"

"…promise never to tell about the black widow safari."

"…promise never to tell about the black widow safari."

"If I do the Devil will make my mother's hair fall out."

"What?"

"You heard me, Eric. Do you want in or not?"

"It's just that I don't want the Devil around my mom."

"Are you planning to tell someone?"

"No…"

"Then you don't have anything to worry about. There's a reason for this, Eric. You're not very good at keeping secrets and this will help you."

"Okay," said Eric. "If I do the Devil will make my mother's hair fall out."

"That wasn't so bad, was it?" asked Doug.

We walked down our long overgrown driveway and ran right into my twelve-year-old brother, Steve. Before we could stop him, Eric blurted out, "Guess what, Steve? We're going to catch ten black widow spiders and dump them on a red ant hill. Isn't that neat?"

My brother then treated us to the words we least liked to hear: "YOU GUYS ARE TOO YOUNG!"

Boy, I hated those words. Steve told us we were too young to catch black widow spiders, but agreed it sounded like a great idea. He offered to catch the spiders for us, and if we were good he would let us hold the jar.

As we followed my brother to our backyard, I held up my fist to Eric and said, "I'm never going to tell you a secret again. I hope you're thinking about what you just did to your mother, you oathbreaker."

I sadly handed over the catching stick to my brother and Doug reluctantly handed the peanut butter jar to me. Eric was trying to visualize his mother bald and wondering if she would know that it was his fault.

It took only a minute to discover the first spider. She was residing behind our tool shed. Her web was spun between the fence and the shed and bore the evidence of many a successful hunt. The dried bodies of three moths and two flies were mute reminders of her deadly capacities.

We crowded behind Steve to watch him catch the first of the ten spiders. He managed to get her on the end of the stick and called for me to open the jar. With trembling hands I opened the jar, and with a tap of the stick it received its first prisoner. She was medium-sized and looked none too happy about being caught. She looked just like the spider on the pamphlet, and when I lifted the jar we were able to see the bright red hourglass on her shiny black abdomen.

As the jar began to fill up, my job became more and more difficult. The fifth spider attached a web to the lid so that when I opened the jar for the sixth spider I pulled the fifth across my hand.

After we had caught eight spiders we faced a dilemma. We ran out of spiders to catch on our property. Steve wanted to stop at eight, but I insisted that since we had agreed to catch ten that's exactly the number we should catch. Steve gave in, but he had no idea as to where we should hunt next. Eric, who had been the quiet observer on the safari, made a great suggestion: "I bet the evil queen of the black widow spiders lives in Mrs. Brown's greenhouse." Mrs. Brown lived next door to Doug, and all the neighborhood children were really afraid of her. She hated small children and would call the police on them if they even set foot on her property. Some of us were convinced that she was a witch and could cast spells that could keep us under her power and things like that.

What made Eric's idea so attractive was that catching the spiders had become too easy and besides, my brother Steve was having all the fun. It was such a great idea that Eric was forgiven for breaking the oath and we told him so. He said he was glad because he couldn't get used to the idea of having a bald mother. He said the thought it might be embarrassing.

Doug suggested that we sneak onto Mrs. Brown's property from his backyard. Her greenhouse was in the very back of her backyard, so Doug's suggestion was taken. We peered over Doug's fence into the untrimmed jungle that made up her yard and concluded that she was not outside. One at a time we dropped into forbidden territory and slipped silently into the greenhouse.

It was damp and dark, musty and moldy—perfect for black widows. We all felt that Mrs. Brown would jump out and grab us at any minute, so we asked Eric to keep watch.

Underneath her gardening bench was a five-gallon red clay pot. It was the kind my mother used to pot a small palm tree. It was turned upside down and resting on three red bricks. Steve and Doug turned it over very slowly and carefully. We each drew in our breath at what we saw. At the bottom of that clay pot was the largest black widow we had ever seen. She was fat and seemed to be throbbing with poison. She was protecting her silky white egg sac, and unlike the other spiders, she was simply not afraid of the stick.

After considerable effort, Steve was able to get the deadly giant on the end of the stick. He called for me to open the jar. I shook the jar until I was able to count the eight spiders we had already captured. Carefully, I turned the lid and removed it from the jar. I stood there with trembling hands while Steve brought the stick to the mouth of the jar. Just at the moment he was going to tap she made a jump for it. She landed right between my bare feet. I backed away, and in the excitement I forgot to put the lid back on the jar. My full attention was directed to the escapee between my feet, and I watched with rapt attention as my brother struggled to get her on the stick.

I failed to notice that a medium-sized female was crawling out of the jar and onto the back of my hand. Slowly, I became aware of an eerie sensation and stared in disbelief at the little killer that was taking a morning stroll on my hand. I let the jar slip through my fingers, and black widows began to run everywhere. They mattered little anymore. The game was over. I was unable to speak words that had meaning but managed a pretty good sound. I believe that phonetically it sounded a little like "yaaaaaaAAAAAAAAAA!" My brother looked at me and it was clear that he was experiencing fear also.

Now I believe that our fear was of different natures. The fear that I was experiencing was because for the first time in my life I really believed that I was going to die. Not like in Cowboys and Indians where you could get up again, but the sort of death where everything goes dark, and after that I wasn't sure what would happen. It took all my strength to keep from fainting. I could feel every footfall of the spider on the back of my hand. I stayed perfectly still.

I begged my brother with my tear-filled eyes to please get the spider off my hand. He moved his index finger in a flicking position to within an inch of the spider. I held my breath and wanted to close my eyes, but I was afraid that if I did it would be for the last time. The spider stopped as if to consider what threat the finger was going to pose, and when she did, Steve flicked with all his might. The spider went flying. I have never felt a greater sense of relief in my life. Neither have I before or since learned a more important truth: someday I am going to die.

How you feel about that truth has everything to do with how you prepare for it. If you have no belief in God or a future existence, then it really doesn't matter how you live your life. On the other hand, if you do believe in God, then everything you do matters. The Bible has two verses that really intrigue me:

> ...it is appointed for men to die once and after this comes judgment...
>
> Hebrews 9:27

We were designed to die. To die once is part of what being a man is all about. We have an appointment with death and nothing we can do will make us early or late. Listen to what James has to say concerning his view of life and death.

> Come now, you who say, "Today or tomorrow, we shall go to such and such a city, and spend a year there and engage in business and make a profit." Yet you do not know what your life will be like tomorrow. You are just a vapor that appears for a little while and vanishes away. Instead you ought to say, "If the Lord wills we shall live and do this or that."
>
> James 4:13–15

The Scripture clearly teaches that there is a God, and what we do matters a great deal to Him. It is also clear that whatever it is that we're going to accomplish needs to be accomplished before we die. The wisest man who ever lived wrote a dissertation on his search for truth and wisdom. His final words and conclusions are as follows:

> The end of the matter; all has been heard. Fear God and keep His commandments; for this is the whole duty of man. For God will bring every deed into judgment, with every secret thing, whether good or evil.
>
> Ecclesiastes 12:13–14

Counting The Cost

When I was young my father told me to always count the cost. It was good but wasted advice. I didn't know how. I had too little experience with life and too much pride to ask anyone who had seen the price tags. Looking back, I'm fairly sure that if someone had given me their cost estimate, I would have thought I could get it for less.

I think this flaw is inherent in humanity, especially the young, and is also the reason why the German philosopher Hegel wrote, "The only thing we've learned from history is that we have learned nothing from history."

I remember the oral interviews I took to become an animal keeper. I was twenty-three years old. A salty old veteran of hundred, maybe thousands, of interviews looked at me over his rimless glasses and asked, "You've told us what you think will be the fun parts of working at the zoo. What do you think will be some of the difficulties or unpleasantries?"

Never having worked at a zoo, I didn't have a clue. I had so romanticized zoo work that I couldn't think of anything bad. I had to say something, so I blurted out, "I guess I'll go home with my clothes smelling bad sometimes."

He looked at me meditatively. His expression said, "If you

want to say more you can." But I couldn't think of anything more, so he broke the awkward silence and the interview continued.

I worked at the zoo for seven years, and all the good things that I had anticipated were a part of the package. But there were also costs...some very high costs. Let me share a few.

There were assaults on my dignity. The first animal to attack me was a small, very huffy male penguin that resented being chased out of a bunker onto exhibit. I was nearly kicked to death by an ostrich that was insulted when I failed to respond to his romantic advances. I was assigned to give a tetanus shot to a wild donkey that had stepped on a rusty nail. When I administered the shot to his flank, he returned the favor by kicking me so hard I almost went through the barn door. I can still feel his "shot" on rainy days.

I was inches from being gored to death by a kudu, a large African antelope. He had mistaken me for a rival suitor. Later this same seven-hundred-pound herd bull did plunge his thirty-six-inch horns through another keeper's body. I was nipped by a rabid raccoon and had to go through the painful series of shots in the stomach. They were worse than I had imagined. I nearly died from the treatment (3 percent of the patients who undergo the Pasteur treatment die from it). I was consistently exposed to zoonosis, diseases transmissible from animals to man, many of which could prove to be fatal.

When I spoke out on behalf of the animals because of poor conditions, I was sent to the zoo's version of Siberia. The section to which I was assigned had more work than a man could do well in eight hours, and most men who were sent there had quit with broken spirits. I discovered that I was allergic to dust and hay, and this section had more of both than any other section in the zoo. I developed chronic bronchitis and drifted into pneumonia on several occasions.

Oh, yes—and there were days when my clothes did smell bad, even terrible.

This is a very partial list, but I think you get the idea. I know something now for sure that was theoretical many years ago when I was hoping to work at the zoo. Anything really valuable has a price tag. M. Scott Peck's opening words in *The Road Less Traveled* are so very true:

> Life is difficult. This is a great truth, one of the greatest truths. It is a great truth because once we truly see this truth, we transcend it. Once we truly know that life is difficult—once we truly understand and accept it—then life is not longer difficult. Because once it is accepted, the fact that life is difficult no longer matters.

Life at its best will cost us something, and life lived at its best is lived for Jesus Christ. Jesus knows the price tag because He paid the price. Let's remember what He said:

> ...If anyone wishes to come after Me, let him deny himself, and take up his cross, and follow Me. For whoever wishes to save his life shall lose it; and whoever loses his life for My sake and the gospel's shall save it. For what does it profit a man to gain the whole world and forfeit his soul?
>
> Mark 8:34–37

Paul spoke plainly when he wrote to the Philippians:

> For to you it has been granted for Christ's sake, not only to believe in Him, but also to suffer for His sake.
>
> Philippians 1:29

So as I read it, the cost is dying to ourselves and believing and being willing to suffer. Well, it's the least we can do for Him. He's done it for us. And we didn't even deserve it.

Think about these questions: What is my faith costing me? How am I demonstrating the value of my Lord, my family, and my church to the world around me? And why did the Lord think I was worth the price He paid for me?

As my father said, "You should always count the cost." I know what you mean now, Dad. I really do.

THE INTERVENTION

I couldn't say I hadn't been warned. I had been…and by the most respected keeper at the zoo. He had walked right up to me two months before and said, "Richmond, anybody tell you about the kudu?" (A kudu is an extremely large, six-hundred-pound antelope with horns that spiral thirty-six inches above its head. It is tan and white with soft vertical stripes on its muscular sides. The females are more delicate and have no horns.)

"No, Jack," I responded. "Is there something I should know?"

"Be careful," he said matter-of-factly. Then he walked back to his section.

No one knew more about African hoofstock than Jack Badal. He had been given the Marlin Perkins Award for his amazing accomplishments with hoofstock. So if he said I should be careful, then careful I would be.

I did a little research and discovered that the male kudu becomes sexually mature at two years. Our male had just reached that milestone. Smaller sixty-pound antelopes can become a bit dangerous during breeding season, but a six-hundred-pound greater kudu could be lethal. Even lions avoided such an animal.

I began to watch and noticed some very subtle changes. First, the kudu began to withdraw from human contact. Then he took to sharpening his horns on the granite walls of his compound. I watched him carefully, knowing of his potential.

When I worked this section I would arrive at the zoo at 4:45 a.m. and check my animals. If anything happened during the night, I wanted to be the one who discovered it. If everything checked out, I would spend the next hour reading at the golf course clubhouse adjacent to the zoo, then begin my 6:00 a.m. to 2:30 p.m. schedule.

I'll never forget a June morning in 1968. It was an hour before sunrise and very foggy. The zoo is eerie when it's dark and downright scary when the fog is draping the streetlights and muffling the sounds. I walked by the impala and noticed that they were standing with their ears cocked toward the kudu barn. Henry, the saddle-bill stork, was pacing. Normally he would be on one leg asleep. Something was up! I hurried my pace.

When I reached the kudus, my heart was gripped with terror. The male was viciously attacking the females. Unless I was successful in separating them, the females would be killed. I knew what was happening. In the wild the females would be giving off a scent that attracts and provokes the males. The males would fight each other for days; and when the strongest emerged, they would claim the females and mating would begin. In a zoo there are no extra males to fight and the females are not ready to mate. The male becomes enraged when the females reject him and they become the recipients of his wrath.

They were in their night quarters, a small forty-by-forty-foot corral adjacent to where they were put on public display during the day. It was the largest yard in the zoo. I thought the females might live if I was successful in letting them out so they could avoid him. The problem was that in order to let them out, I had to enter and walk completely across the small corral. The male didn't look as if he wanted company. But something had to be done now. I grabbed a rake and shovel and placed them in a wheelbarrow. I unlocked the gate and stepped into the corral. Everything became still…and it seemed as if I had entered a bad dream. The male stared at me and shook his head in challenge. I whistled "Amazing Grace" and began to back across the corral. He stalked me like a cat stalks a mouse. His eyes were full of rage. I finally reached the other side and fumbled for the lock. I turned the key, keeping one eye on the enraged male who was standing fifteen feet in front of me. It clicked and I slid it out of the hasp. The male charged. I could see the finely sharpened tips of his horns headed for my chest. I threw myself against the gate. It gave way and I fell backwards. There was a brown blur, a sickening thud, and a mournful cry. A female had run for the gate and taken my blow. I scrambled up the chain-link gate and cast myself out of the exhibit. I landed on my back seven feet below on a thick bed of ivy where, for several seconds, I pondered the question "Am I alive?" My heart was pounding and I was soaking wet. I took those to be good signs.

After thirty minutes of intense efforts, I was able to separate the male from the females. He was locked in a barn for two weeks and let out when the females were ready for him. Both females gave birth several months later. One of them always wore a scar where the male gored her as he attempted to kill me. Her saving my life had not been intentional, but I always gave her special treatment after that. I loved her for it.

It occurred to me that this was not the first time someone had taken punishment for me. It had happened before, only on that occasion my Savior had known exactly what He was doing and what it would mean.

But He was pierced through for our transgressions. He was crushed for our iniquities; the chastening for our well-being fell upon Him, and by his scourging we are healed.

Isaiah 53:5

Have you thanked Jesus lately? Perhaps it's time you did.

WHAT IF?

I have played the "What If?" game since childhood. You have too, I'll bet. The really great players are blessed or cursed with active imaginations. In a group of people, What If-ers are sure to be the ones who create the most enthusiasm or inspire the most fear.

I began developing my skills when I was very young, and by the fifth grade I was quite capable of What If-ing with the best of them. My friend, Doug, and I had even What If-ed our way into believing there was a Bigfoot creature residing in a nearby canyon. Yes, sir, I am fully convinced that I was What If-ing at high school level—maybe higher.

What If-ing carries with it an awesome power. It is the power of suggestion. The power does not diminish as one gets older. It increases.

By the time I had reached my twenty-fifth year of life I had turned What If-ing into a science. If there were an Olympics for What If-ers I would have been in the decathalon. If there had been Olympics of that type it would have been held at the Los Angeles Zoo. That's where the best What If-ers trained. If you would ever like to see them in training, visit the zoo at breaktime. They will What If like crazy for fifteen minutes out of every twenty minutes of breaktime.

I remember the day that a group of veteran keepers got together for what may be the finest single session of What If-ing in the history of man. It was the summer of 1968. It was really warm for ten o'clock in the morning and the air was crystal clear, which was odd for Los Angeles. The heat brought more keepers than usual who thought an ice-cold soft drink might just hit the spot. We gathered at the North American snack bar and filled the cement picnic tables that circled the building. We enjoyed the shade and the fraternity.

It didn't take long for the conversation to turn into a What If-ing session.

Don got us started. "Did you hear that some hermit has been sneaking into the zoo at night, crawling into exhibits and stealing food from the animals? Guy's nuts, I bet. What if a guy like that got hold of a set of keys? He could let a lot of animals out in a short amount of time."

Dale added, "What if a guy like that got into the reptile house? Can you imagine what Griffith Park would be like with cobras and mambas and all sorts of vipers? You couldn't get anybody to come to the zoo for years. There'd be a big lawsuit if anybody got bit. You could count on that."

"What if that guy let Bosco the cape buffalo out? Cape buffalos have knocked boxcars off train tracks in Africa. I'd hate to come into the zoo some morning and find Bosco looking at me. He charges the fence now. Can you image what fun he'd have really knocking people around like beach balls? Did you ever watch him stand behind his fence and go into a rage? He trembles and salivates, moans and groans, and then he charges. I swear someday he won't have to wait to be let out. He's going to knock his fence down or come through the side of the barn. That Bosco is something, all right."

John decided it was his moment and spoke. "Ivan's the one that gives me nightmares. What if some nutball let him out?" We all got real quiet because John had just verbalized everybody's worst nightmare. Ivan the polar bear was the most feared animal at the zoo. John seized the opportunity to run with the moment he had created.

"I was here the day Ivan killed Nanatchka. She was a pretty bear. Ivan went right after her. That's just what he'd do to us, you know." John paused again for effect. Everybody stayed silent as they nursed their own private fears of Ivan. John resumed his manipulation. "Bears don't kill you right off."

All the keepers but one left breaktime glad that they didn't have to care for Ivan. Ivan's keeper was a little slow leaving the picnic tables, and he thought about Ivan all the way back to the elephant seal pool. That "he" was me. What made John's What If more effective was the fact that only days before, one of the Kodiak bears had lifted his guillotine door and let all the other Kodiak bears out on exhibit just seconds after the keeper had finished cleaning. He'd be dead for sure if that bear had made his move any sooner. I wondered if Ivan could ever figure out how to open the door and let himself out.

Jim was a relief keeper, and on the way back from break I had discovered that he had been assigned to help me with my string. I had been busy acid-washing the elephant seal pool and was sadly behind. Ivan's exhibit had not been cleaned and neither were the penguins and pelicans on exhibit.

"Al Franklin asked me to clean Ivan's exhibit for you. He said you were behind because of acid-washing. I know the routine, so you don't have to show me anything."

"Thanks, Jim. I owe you one."

"Don't mention it."

Jim headed for the polar bear moat and I went to the pelagic bird exhibit. I remembered that Jim had looked very impressed by John's dissertation and it gave me an idea. Keepers are incurable practical jokers, and they specialize in scare jokes. I knew the cleaning routine for the polar bear moat backwards and forwards. I had performed it hundreds of times myself. Jim would just now be opening up the back door to the moat. He would prop that door open to ventilate the area and walk forward five steps to unlock a sliding door. He would pull it open and slide it shut again. He would turn and look at Ivan who was already looking at him. He would be impressed by the size of Ivan's massive paws. Ivan weighed nine hundred and fifty pounds. He stood nearly ten feet tall. He was 100 percent nightmare and never missed a chance to swipe at a keeper. Ivan was above all things a killer. Jim would lock the guillotine door handle into place so that no one could let Ivan out on him. Then he would open three more chainlink doors that would give him access to the outdoor exhibit. Ivan's pool was already drained, so Jim would grab the one-inch hose, put on the high-pressure nozzle, and turn on the water. The surge of pressure would jar his arm and the noise inside the grotto would be deafening. He would then drag the hose down the dimly lit hallway. He would pull it out into the morning sun and begin cleaning the exhibit.

I timed it so that I was silently entering the back door just as Jim was beginning to clean. I stopped at the hose bib long enough to turn the hose on and off. I makes the guy outside think his hose is kinked and he will give it a dynamic tug to relieve the problem. After doing that a couple of times, I proceeded to stalk my prey down the dimly lit hallway. All I had to do was to follow the hose. As I crept up behind him I could see that he was completely involved with his task. This was going to be too easy. I stepped to within reach of my prey and let out a mighty roar. Now polar bears don't roar, but even the finest keeper would have forgotten that fact under the circumstances. I simultaneously grabbed his shoulder and side. I had never seen anybody try to climb a high-pressure hose before. But that day I did. I'll have to give Jim credit for one thing, He never let go of the hose through all the animation that he achieved. Boy, was he angry. People sometimes get that way when you get them to abandon their dignity. Jim was a soft-spoken man, but he said some words that I had never heard before or since.

Jim had been set up by the negative power of suggestion. What If-ing had taken its toll. Because we are fallen creatures we are prone to think negatively. Our What If-ing mechanisms turned inward usually create apprehension and fear. We become victims of our own thinking patterns. If we allow that to happen, we become cowards, too afraid to make a move—any move—for fear we might fail. Our imagination has the potential to extend our faith or destroy it.

What If-ing prevented two million Israelites from entering the Promised Land. Joshua and Caleb believed God, but everyone else forgot that the Lord would fight for them. Their imaginations took over.

Moses described the effect of What If-ers in Deuteronomy 1:28–33:

> "Whither are we going up? Our brethren have made our hearts melt, saying, 'The people are greater and taller than we; the cities are great and fortified up to heaven; and moreover we have seen the sons of the Anakim there.' Then I said to you, 'Do not be in dread

or afraid of them. The LORD your God who goes before you will himself fight for you, just as he did for you in Egypt before your eyes, and in the wilderness, where you have seen how the LORD your God bore you, as a man bears his son, in all the way that you went until you came to this place.' Yet in spite of this word you did not believe the LORD your God, who went before you in the way to seek you out a place to pitch your tents, in fire by night, to show you by what way you should go, and in the cloud by day.

Gideon hesitated before his heroic acts by speculating that God might have left him. He was asking "What if God decides not to stay by my side?"

We have heard it said, "A coward dies a thousand deaths, a brave man just one."

Romans 12 tells us that we should "renew our minds that we may prove what is the will of God." We must change our way of thinking so that it conforms to God's will.

Negative: What if I share my faith in Christ with that person and they think I'm a fruitcake or a religious nut?

Positive: What if I share my faith with that person? Maybe they will come to know Him and find peace, joy, and salvation.

Negative: What if I said no? Maybe he'd think I was a prude. Maybe he wouldn't ask me out anymore.

Positive: What if I said no? I'd keep my self-respect. And if he doesn't ask me out again, God will provide better.

What If-ing is in its negative context nothing more than worry. And we are commanded not to worry.

> Have no anxiety about anything, but in everything by prayer and supplication with thanksgiving let your requests be made known to God. And the peace of God, which passes understanding, will keep your hearts and minds in Christ Jesus.
>
> Philippians 4:6–7

How do we change if we are worriers (and I am)? It's a matter of forcing ourselves into new ways of thinking. Philippians 4:8 give us a formula:

> Finally, brethren, whatever is true, whatever is honorable, whatever is just, whatever is pure, whatever is lovely, whatever is gracious, if there is any excellence, if there is anything worthy of praise, think about these things.

"But, Lord, what if I can't"

"No excuses, my child! I will be with you."

Badal

There are some men who are larger than life. Jack Badal is such a man.

I remember my first day as a new keeper at the Los Angeles Zoo. I was introduced to the chief keeper who in turn introduced me to one of his principal keepers. The principal keeper was responsible for one-half of the zoo's animal care and would that day introduce me to my senior keeper. Seniors are in charge of a section of exhibits, and keepers are in charge of what we call a "string."

The principal took a moment to size me up and began his introductory speech. "Richmond, there's a right way, a wrong way, and Jack Badal's way to do everything. But only Jack can do it his way, so you just work on getting it right."

Sensing that he had just shared something important, I seized the opportunity to insert a question. "Who is Jack Badal?"

"Jack works African hoofstock just up the road. If you see a man that wears a green baseball cap backwards, whistles while he works, and looks like he could have eaten a Sherman tank for breakfast, that is Jack Badal. He is real particular about who he talks to, and if he doesn't like you he won't talk to you at all. He knows more than anyone here and works harder, too."

"He sounds like an interesting guy. I'll be looking forward to meeting him," I said with enthusiasm.

"Amazing is a better word, I think," added the principal. "And by the way, don't bother asking him any questions about the animals. He won't answer them anyway."

"Why not?"

"Jack is from a different era. He's from the old school, and school of trade secrets. In the old days the keepers were divided into two groups; zookeepers and animal men. The zookeepers basically cleaned and fed wild animals. The animal men turned zookeeping into an art. The animal men knew what their animals were thinking, what they were feeling. They knew what to do to keep them from fighting and from becoming diseased. They knew how to encourage breeding. But they wouldn't pass their knowledge on because their knowledge was their job security. It was valuable, not to be given away just because someone asked for it. Their knowledge had been obtained through careful observation over a long period of time. So why should they give it away?"

I was assigned to the Eurasian section on the opposite side of the zoo from the African hoofstock. I didn't see Jack Badal for three weeks but I heard about him often. When people spoke about Jack, it was usually with awe bordering on reverence. All of the veteran keepers from the old Griffith Park Zoo had Badal stories. I remember hearing that he had single-handedly moved an adult ostrich into a crate for shipment after four men had failed in their joint attempt. I heard that Jack leaped off of a seven-foot wall and subdued a young buffalo so that the zoo vet could give it antibiotics.

One of the favorite stories that circulated for all seven years of my career concerned a strong disagreement. Jack had had it with another keeper who had lied about him, causing him to be accused of something he hadn't done. When Jack confronted him, the man was flippant and smart-mouthed. It apparently angered Jack so that he clenched his fists and considered taking a poke at the sarcastic troublemaker. The man knew he had stepped over a foolish line and looked terrified as Jack stood there shaking with anger. Jack had reached a point that required the release of inner tensions, so he hit the wall right next to the man's head. They say his fist passed through the wall into the next room. Jack stared into the shaken man's eyes for a moment and then left the room.

I'm not sure whether the stories were true or false. Perhaps they were half true. What was true was that Jack was a legend, and people are always adding to legends. Everyone agreed that Jack was our zoo's only animal man, maybe even the last animal man around.

Two years into my career I was assigned to be Jack's relief keeper, which meant that I would take care of Jack's string on his days off. I found my heart beating rapidly when my new senior keeper introduced me to Jack as his new relief man. When the senior keeper left, Jack broke the ice by asking, "Do you like African hoofstock?"

"I'm not sure, I've never worked them before. I want to learn everything I can while I'm at the zoo. It will be great working with you. I hear you're the best. Most of the guys think you're a legend."

Jack smiled and said, "Well you know what they say, 'A legend's feet are made of sand.'"

I knew right away that I was going to enjoy working with Jack. The man turned out to be twice as good as the legend.

"Follow me," he said as he led me to the sable antelope barn. Before we entered the barn he paused quietly at the fence and studied every one of the perfect specimens. His eyes searched quickly for anything that would tip him off to a need or problem. His animals were thriving. Their coats shone in the morning sun and they held their heads proudly. Their eyes had a special sparkle and their muscles rippled with energy. These antelope were neither too fat nor too thin, and their condition was the result of perfect care.

"These sable are really something," he said with quiet admiration. "The males have been know to kill lions. See this fence?" He pointed to the gate. It was bowed out as if it had been hit by a car. "That's where the bull hit the other day trying to get to a passerby. We don't go in with these guys."

I was glad. Jack looked at me to make sure that I was listening. I nodded that I had understood not to go in with these majestic creations with the deadly horns.

I had heard that Jack's barns were so immaculate you could eat your lunch off the floors. I'm sure the statement was true, but I never found the will to test it. He opened the door for my first look and I stepped inside. My eyes searched every corner, especially the stalls. After what he said about the sable antelope I wanted to be sure that we wouldn't be entering any area that was already occupied. All the animals were outside the barn on exhibit. My inspection ended with eye-to-eye contact with Jack. He had been watching me.

"You have the eyes of an animal man," he said.

"Why do you say that?" I asked.

"When we came into the barn you looked into every corner to see what was happening. That's what an animal man does. An animal man doesn't miss a thing. He checks everything out. You're going to be good if you stick with this business."

I counted that as the greatest compliment that I had received at the zoo. Coming from Jack those were most encouraging words.

Jack trained me for two days and I can honestly say that I learned more that had practical value in those sixteen hours than I had learned in the previous two years at the zoo. Jack had turned little things into an art. Raking, for instance, became a subject for learning. He showed me how to position the angle of the rake for greater efficiency. I was able to cut my raking time in half. He showed me a technique for tossing dirt back through the rake tines while retaining the leaves and waste material. He showed me how to sculpture the yard to improve rain drainage. He packed the dirt down firmly and kept it from being dusty with frequent waterings. The end result was animals with clear lungs and hooves that seemed to wear down at just the perfect rate. I can't recall our ever needing to trim the hooves of any of the animals on Jack's string. Jack taught me to whistle while I worked. I felt like a dwarf now and then, but my animals never needed to watch for me if they could hear where in the exhibit I was. This practice really did relieve tension. Jack showed me a way to moisten the hay so that it was more enjoyable for the animals. He also showed me how to place the hay in different locations so that competition for the food was reduced. I found Jack to be colorful, knowledgeable, efficient, and a great storyteller; he was the hardest worker I have ever met and a dedicated Christian.

I asked Jack to explain his philosophy of animal keeping. His answers were thought-provoking. He said, "Gary, I try to spend each day at the zoo so that I never regret yesterday. These animals provide a job for me. With the pay I get I give to God and I feed my family. I figure I owe the animals the best I can give. It's my job to take all the bad things out of their world and replace them with good things. They depend on me and I don't want to let them down."

Proverbs 12:10 always comes to my mind when I think of Jack.

"A righteous man has regard for the life of his beast."

Jack was a living proverb. I did and still do consider Jack Badal the best in the business—the last of the great animal men.

Jack's skills were not limited to animal care. He was also one of the greatest animal trainers in history. He trained elephants for the zoo, and was especially fond of a lowland gorilla named Ramar. That gorilla performed tricks gorillas had never been taught before. Jack loved that animal, and his eyes sparkled whenever I asked him about Ramar. The day that Ramar became too large to be safely controlled came all too soon. I know that it broke Jack's heart to give him up to an eastern zoo, but it had to be done.

One of my favorite stories is one that Jack told me about how he became the trainer for the Los Angeles Zoo. They needed someone to train the elephants to walk the two miles to the new zoo. Three men applied.

"Gary, they brought the three of us candidates into a waiting room and told us to please sit down. Animal trainers are a funny breed, and we didn't talk much while we were waiting for our turn to be interviewed. They called the first guy in and about two minutes later we heard a macaw squawking his head off. In another two minutes the first guy comes out. He's red-faced and doesn't say a word. He just leaves in a huff. He second guy goes in and the same thing happens again, only the bird is even louder than before. Number two comes out shaking his head, looks at me, rolls his eyes, and leaves. I wondered what was going on.

" 'Mr. Badal, would you please come in?' asked one of the interviewers. I said 'Yes, sir,' and walked right into the room. There were some important men from city hall, and the zoo directors, of course. Right in the middle of the room was a large cage with a very nervous scarlet macaw. He was looking at everybody and rocking back and forth because he was still upset.

"The director said, 'So you want to be our trainer, Mr. Badal?'

" 'Yes, sir,' I answered.

" 'We would like to get a little idea of your skills, Mr. Badal.' They handed me a small bird net with about a two-foot handle and asked me if I would please take the macaw out of the cage for them.

"I knew just what had been happening. The two guys ahead of me were manhandling the bird. They had most likely netted the bird, drug him out of the cage, and put him back in. That's why the bird was so upset. I hid the net behind my back and spoke quietly to the bird until I could see that he was calming down. Then I slowly and carefully opened the door and let him get used to that. I turned the net around and offered the handle to the bird. He stepped right on and I lifted him out of the cage slowly and stood before the interview board.

"I said, 'Now what would you like me to do with the bird?'

" 'Put him back in the cage, Mr. Badal. And congratulations— you are our new trainer.'"

In Jack's world he is the standard of excellence, admired by his peers and respected by his friends. He is the kind of person about whom it is said, "They don't make them like that anymore." As great as all of his accomplishments in the animal world are, they are excelled by the quality of his walk with Jesus Christ. You see, Jack lives his life according to Colossians 3:17:

> And whatever you do, in word or deed, do everything
> in the name of the Lord Jesus, giving thanks to God the
> Father through him.

BOBCAT

Since early childhood, I have suffered under the illusion that if I could obtain a certain possession or experience, I would be fulfilled, completed, happy. I am now decades past childhood and you would think I would have wisened and grown beyond these periodic wanderings into fantasyland. But I have not.

The smell of a new car, the shiny cover of a new book, the high-resolution picture screen on a television, the sleek lines of a new camera—all these things call to me like sirens of old called to sailors to steer their sailing ships into certain oblivion. For me, fighting these urges might compare to a reformed smoker's desire to light one up or a recovered alcoholic's desire to feel the warmth of whiskey as it sears the throat and settles into the system.

My *needs* have always been met, but never my *wants*. My wants seem endless. You would know that if you had ever watched me come alive leafing through a Sears catalog—one of my favorite pastimes.

I have had some strange wants fulfilled and am grieved to report that I was never ever made happy by them. In fact, they are now an embarrassment to me. Let me tell you the worst-case scenario. It happened many years ago and still has a humbling effect whenever I recall it.

As a sophomore at Los Angeles Pacific College, I was living in a small one-bedroom apartment with two very stable and godly young men who were both seniors at the same Christian college. I was engaged to Carol, my bride of almost four decades now. Those who knew me then thought of me as a responsible, thoughtful and dedicated young man. However, those who knew me well knew I was capable of some unusual behavior.

It was during that period that I decided that the purchase of a bobcat would make me happy. It did not.

For weeks, I combed the classified section of the *Los Angeles Times* under the heading "Exotic Pets," hoping to see bobcat kittens for sale. One Friday afternoon I did find an ad, and my heart leapt for joy within me. My fingers trembled with anticipation as I dialed the phone number that was listed.

A woman answered and confirmed all my imaginings—that bobcats were indeed the new wave of the pet trade. She adored her female, and I could hardly take down directions to their home fast enough because she had only two kittens left.

I rushed down as fast as I could to find that the young kittens had been sold. But the couple again lifted my spirits by telling me that they had a teenaged bobcat on their back porch, which they would be willing to part with at a bargain price. Under the spell of having an unusual pet, I did not notice that their house smelled like a giant, unchanged kitty litter box.

As I held their pet, a very affectionate adult female, I was certain beyond any doubt that a bobcat is what I wanted—i.e., had to have! They took me to the back porch and there in a small carrying cage was a nearly-grown female. When she saw me, she snarled and hissed. Her ears went down and she glared and growled the whole time we were there talking.

The man assured me, "She'll tame down fine (LIAR!). She just doesn't like being in a small cage like that." Did I mention that the man looked like he could be Anton LeVey's brother?

This wasn't what I had driven forty miles to buy, but she would tame down. Well, at least the bobcat looked healthy—or maybe just possessed! I paid $125 and left thinking what fun it would be to own a tame wildcat. I named her Tara. It seemed exotic and wild and fit perfectly.

When I finally got to our apartment, I was sad neither of my roommates was there to enjoy the surprise. I let the cat out of the carrying cage. She ran wildly around the room, searching for a place to escape. She opted to jump from the floor to the kitchen sink, then to a room divider just over the stove, about six feet above the ground. From there, she glared and continued to growl.

She would tame down, he had said (WRONG!). I offered the bobcat assorted parts of an uncooked chicken, but she only batted them away with a haughty, who-needs-it attitude. Well, give her time. Bummer!

I had to leave the apartment to run an errand. That's when my roommate Fred came home, unaware that the apartment was occupied. He innocently walked to the kitchen sink to pour a glass of water. That's when he heard the low, rumbling growl behind him. He turned around slowly and found himself face-to-face with the she-devil bobcat I had purchased for just $125.

Fred backed slowly out of the kitchen, staying as close to the wall and as far away as he could from the evil presence which had claimed our apartment. Beads of perspiration formed all over his face as he let himself out the front door. Art would never get a bobcat, so Fred knew I would be able to unravel the mystery. He waited for me to get home—safe on our porch.

I returned from my errand excited to see Fred sitting on the front porch of our apartment. Something was obviously bothering him, so I asked him what was wrong. He looked at me as if I should know.

"Gary," he began in an exasperated way, "What's in our apartment? I went into get something to drink and eat and began to hear a low, rumbling growl. I looked behind me, and ready to attack was some sort of wild animal. Is that a bobcat in there?"

"Yes, Fred, and she'll tame down soon. The family I bought her from said she's uptight from being in a small carrying cage. I got a great deal on her. She cost only $125."

"Gary, don't you think it would have been good to ask Art and me before getting a bobcat? Personally, I liked our apartment better when I felt safe in it. I don't think it's going to tame down. Don't they call bobcats wildcats?"

"Come on, Fred. Tara will tame down, and you'll love her. Fred, you are so responsible and predictable, you need a little excitement in your life. You'll be able to tell your grandchildren you lived with a bobcat during your college days. Give it a try. Really, what can it hurt?"

We kept eye contact and Fred, a little stung with the idea that he was too responsible and predictable, finally spoke. "Okay, we'll give it a try. If it doesn't work out, you and Tara will have to make other arrangements."

When we stepped into our small apartment, we were greeted by a significant odor. It was a good news/bad news thing. The good news was that Tara had used her kitty litter tray; the bad news was that she needed a tray six times larger and deeper to achieve sanitation. Kitty litter and odor were everywhere. I'm an optimist, but even I knew that this was not a good beginning. Fred didn't say anything but gave me a very skeptical look.

When Art got home, he got a big laugh out of the whole deal and was more willing than Fred to give it a try. He laughed every time it growled at one of us, which it continued to do every day it lived with us, which was a little over a week.

Tara never allowed me to pet her or even touch her. Every effort ended with her taking a fearsome swipe at me, and then she would run and hide behind or under something. Most of the time, though, she just stared down from her favorite haunt—the room divider above the kitchen. Fred and Art locked themselves in the bedroom at night and left me on the couch with Tara lurking somewhere in the darkness. Our apartment smelled like a giant kitty litter box, and it was filled with tension.

Even an optimist usually knows when something isn't working. I knew the guys were anxious for me to admit that living in small quarters with a wild animal was not good. They wanted me to say, "Guys, you were right; this was a stupid thing to do." But I hate to admit it when I'm wrong, so it took a final straw.

Tara somehow got into the bathroom early in the morning when everybody else in the apartment needed to get ready for classes. She claimed it for her own and would not let any of us in for whatever reason. She was getting wilder and meaner each day. Even I was not sure whether or not she would attack. At any rate, all three of us left for class unwashed, unshaven, and undeodorized.

As he left, Fred spoke the words I knew were coming: "She has to go!"

When Art nodded, I shared something really difficult and painful for me to say. "You guys are right. I never should have bought her."

I called the man who sold me Tara; he was sad she wasn't working out. He said he knew a man who wanted her and would send him right over. Man, everything was going to work out fine, I thought. The man showed up and with a little effort—about an hour of terrifying running around—we finally got Tara back into her carrier. I told the man I'd sell her for only $125. He said that was more than a fair price, but he didn't have the money right then and would send it to me.

I didn't have much of a bargaining position, so I let him take the bobcat, which I didn't want any longer anyway. A week passed, but no money came. I called the telephone number he had given me. Guess what? Disconnected. I drove to the address he had given to me; he had been evicted.

My only satisfaction was that he had the bobcat.

And that's the only satisfaction that this story brings me because it highlights one of my greatest weaknesses, one I continue to fight: the subconscious conviction that a certain purchase will make me happy. I was nineteen when all of this occurred. I'm about forty years older now, but there are still times I must fight to keep from being foolish and attempting to fill voids that are not there.

I am wiser now and know one thing for sure: if I live to be one hundred, I will never buy another bobcat.

You Might Have To Ask

Nothing is more frustrating than living with an unsolved mystery. That's how the zoo staff felt when every day at ten o'clock an old man would visit the children's zoo. He was tall and dignified, and his suit, vest, tie, overcoat, and shoes showed signs of considerable age and wear. With a cane in one hand and shopping bag in the other, he would walk to isolated spots in the children's zoo and then look over his shoulders to see if anyone was watching. This, of course, aroused suspicion and the zoo staff began to watch him carefully. The following is what they observed.

He would open his shopping bag and reach in for slices of dry bread, which he scattered about the bench where he was seated. He then adjusted his pant legs and started pulling what seemed to be threads or something out from under his cuff. Wild ground squirrels would gather to eat the bread, and when they did he would leap up from the bench and raise his arms high in the air. On some occasions he would pound his lower legs and then retire to the men's room. At other times he would readjust his pant legs and begin to pull at the threads again. By noon, he was gone.

The old man was driving the staff crazy. And his behavior became the object of much conversation and theory, none of which was kind. He was labeled the "kook," the "pervert," and was thought to be strange. Some even wondered if he was safe around children.

His activities were brought to the attention of our director. Being a man unable to live with mystery, he watched the man through binoculars for several minutes, but was unable to determine what he was doing. He decided to take a direct approach, so he confronted the old gentleman personally.

"What are you doing, sir?" said the director. "You are driving the staff crazy." The old man, his head bowed, quietly explained. "I live on a fixed income, you see, and I can't afford much food, especially meat. My doctor says I need protein so I'm squirrel fishing. I pass fishing line down my pant legs and put chunks of bread on treble hooks. When the squirrels reach for the bread..."

The director raised his hand to stop the old gentleman from saying more. He could see the man looked humiliated. "To tell you the truth," said the director, "those squirrels are pests and you're probably helping us. It's just that if some child sees you...well, I think you understand." The director then took out his wallet and pressed ten dollars into the old man's wrinkled hand. "This is for hamburgers, okay?" The old man nodded gratefully, then left. We never saw him again.

It is so easy to think the worse, to make the wrong assumption. If people don't smile much or cease to talk to me, I rarely think to ask them why. I am ten times more likely to assign a wrong meaning to their silence. Often my last thought is that their silence may be the loudest cry for help that they are capable of making.

The apostle Paul once wrote:

> Do nothing from selfishness or conceit, but with humility of mind let each of you regard one another as more important than himself; do not merely look out

for your own personal interest, but also for the interests of others.

Philippians 2:3–4

Is anybody in your life behaving strangely? Maybe it's time to ask what's going on.

MIRROR, MIRROR

Nobody knew why Ivan wouldn't come in to eat. His voracious appetite had pulled him through the guillotine door for twenty years of zoo life. But there he stood, just outside the door, staring through everything, into infinity. This nine-hundred-and-fifty-pound polar bar had never missed a day of eating. Food was his life. I threw him a mackerel and it landed still inside the night quarters just four feet from his face. He continued staring into space.

"Come on, Ivan. I want to go home," I pleaded.

No amount of coaxing made any difference whatsoever. I didn't have the authority to leave him outside, so I ran to get Al Franklin, my senior keeper. Al had worked with Ivan for a lot longer than I had and might have known a trick to bring him in.

Al tried all the same things that I had tried but with no more success than I had achieved.

"Did you ever drop a door on Ivan?" he asked.

"No, Al, I never have," I answered. We had a good friendship and there was no reason to believe he would doubt my word.

Al didn't have the authority to leave Ivan on exhibit overnight. So he called Fred Rose, the chief keeper, who did have the authority. Fred's first question was, "Did anybody drop a door on

Ivan?" and Al assured him that neither he nor I had done so. Fred felt that Ivan should be locked on exhibit without food till morning and hunger would be our best bet to bring him in.

Morning came all too soon and we resumed our efforts to bring in the bear. Still no success. The problem his obstinance was creating was that we could not clean his outdoor quarters unless we could lock him inside. The zoo's architect had placed the drain valve to Ivan's large swimming pool inside the exhibit with the most dangerous bear in the zoo.

Ivan was also the messiest bear in the zoo. It was summertime and by the end of the second day his pool was becoming light green with free-floating algae. The third day the algae began to settle on the sides of the pool and the exhibit began to smell musky and sulphurous.

The fourth day we tried something clever. We tied a live chicken to the bars inside his cage and let it walk about. We hoped that it would stimulate his feeding instincts, but it didn't.

We would have tranquilized him but there was a terrific chance that he would stumble into his pool and drown. Actually, there were some of us who thought we would be willing to take that chance.

After a week had passed, you could smell Ivan's exhibit as soon as you entered the aquatics section—it smelled like a sewer! Every supervisor in the zoo began suggesting things we had already tried and asked whether I had dropped the door on Ivan's head. I suspected that someone had done that in the past, causing Ivan to fear going near the door for a period of time. But I couldn't think of anything I had done that might have caused this strange behavior on Ivan's part.

One week stretched into two, then three. Ivan hadn't eaten for twenty-one days, but we made sure he had fresh water daily by directing the stream from a high pressure hose near his massive head. The weather was uncomfortably hot and Ivan was glad for a good cooling off. We had no idea how long it would be before we won the battle of wills, because fat polar bears are capable of going incredible periods of time without food if they have access to water.

On the twenty-second day. Al Franklin found me by the sea lion exhibit and asked me if I would help him. He told me he had gotten an idea that just might work. I had long since become skeptical, but I was amazed that there was a new idea to try.

Al said, "Follow me to the men's room at the chief's shack and I'll show you my idea." I couldn't begin to imagine what there could be in the men's room that might lure Ivan into his night quarters. But my curiosity was at an all-time high.

Al led me into the men's room and proudly pointed to the four-by-five-foot mirror mounted over the two porcelain washbasins. I knew I was missing something because for the life of me nothing about the mirror struck me as having the capacity for catching a nine-hundred-and-fifty-pound polar bear. I began to wonder if I was missing a philosophical approach like "the answer is inside ourselves" or something like that. Ivan was not a vain bear, and a mirror would not service his needs at all. Why, he didn't even own a brush or a comb.

"Okay, Al, I'm sure this is going to be good, but I just can't see it. How is the mirror going to help us?"

"Ivan has killed two other polar bears, right?" he said.

"Right."

"So the way I've got it figured, he hates other bears. If we prop this mirror up just behind his bars on the outside, he'll look in and think he is seeing another bear. It will make him madder than fire and he'll run in to kill it. Anyway, that's my theory."

"It's worth a try," I said, as we began unscrewing the mounts that held the mirror to the wall. We carried the mirror into the back of the bear grotto and leaned it into position so that when opened the guillotine door Ivan would be staring at his own reflection.

Al stepped aside so that Ivan would see nothing but a bear in the dim light of the night quarters. I lifted the door and peered cautiously at our stubborn nightmare. He was instantly aroused by the bear in the mirror and moaned quietly. He rocked back and forth and then charged the bear in the mirror aggressively. As soon as he cleared the door I dropped it into place. Al had found the answer. We got a lot of good laughs because of the unorthodox nature of the capture, but everyone admired Al for his original thinking.

One of the ways man is different from the animals is that he realizes he is looking at his own reflection. He has self-realization. We may see an enemy in the mirror, but the enemy may be us. There have been times in my life when looking the mirror was very painful because of how I was living my life. It is strange when you find yourself avoiding your own gaze because you feel that you can't respect the person you have become. Look at what James 1:21–25 has to say:

> Therefore put away all filthiness and rank growth of wickedness and receive with meekness the implanted word, which is able to save your souls. But be doers of the word, and not hearers only, deceiving yourselves. For if any one is a hearer of the word and not a doer, he is like a man who observes his natural face in a mirror; for he observes himself and goes away and at once forgets what he was like. But he who looks into the perfect law, the law of liberty, and perseveres,

being no hearer that forgets but a doer that acts, he shall be blessed in his doing.

Find a mirror. Look deep into your own eyes and say,

Search me, O God, and know my heart! Try me and know my thoughts! And see if there by any wicked way in me, and lead me in the way everlasting.

Psalm 139:23–24

Now do what God tells you. There is peace and joy there.

Sins of the Father

When I was first transferred to the zoo health center I was introduced to the most heartless man I have ever known. It might surprise you, but the man was an animal keeper. He was responsible for the hillside string which included bison, tule elk, peccary, mule deer, axis deer, and a solitary mountain goat. Even though my main duties were in the health center, I became his relief keeper one day a week. I didn't mind hoofstock, in fact I loved them, but since he never did any work the area was always a mess by Friday. The first day we met he told me how proud he was that he was paid so much for so little work. He claimed that he never worked more than one hour a day.

The barns were in a location that gave him an excellent view of any approaching supervisors. He would sit atop the stacks of hay and read pornographic magazines. If anybody approached he would leap off the hay bales and grab a rake and shovel and pretend he had been working. He even went so far as to put water under his armpits so that it would appear that he'd worked up a good sweat. His laziness was disgusting, but it was not that quality which I cared for least. It was his cruelty.

Benedict hated animals, as had his father before him. They would never say that, but their actions yelled louder than their words.

One fine day, when Bambi the male mule deer had grown an impressive four-pointed set of antlers, Benedict decided he would enter the deer's yard. He wished to show off to an attractive college girl who was sketching the deer. During rutting season deer can be very dangerous and very unpredictable. Benedict should have locked Bambi up, but he didn't because he delighted in showing his mastery over the animal.

Benedict was carrying a leaf rake and poked Bambi in the side as he walked by. Bambi's instincts took over and he charged his antagonist. He rammed his antlers into the man's chest and knocked him down the hill. It was a steep hill, and Benedict tumbled sixty feet to the bottom. He was punctured in four places and shaken. When he stood up, the attractive college girl gave him a dirty look and walked away.

Later that day Benedict was quoted as having said, "If it's the last thing I do I'm going to kill that —————— deer!"

Nobody took him seriously, but they should have. As days went by Bambi began to lose weight. His ribs began to show and he would follow anyone who walked by his corral. The vets ordered stool samples to see if Bambi was suffering from parasites, but everything always checked out fine. We later came to believe that the stool samples delivered to us were those of a healthy axis deer next door. Blood was taken and it checked out fine. There was no good reason for the demise of Bambi.

A new keeper was assigned to work Benedict's days off. It was not long until he suspected the deer was not being fed enough to survive. In a compassionate but foolish move he dumped several scoops of herbivore pellets into Bambi's hay manger. Bambi, crazed with hunger, ate all of the pellets. They caused him to become thirsty, and he drank far too much water. Bambi died as a result of acute gastric disturbances.

The new keeper was issued a deficiency notice, and rightly so, but the real culprit went unpunished because nothing could be proven.

When Benedict and I first talked together he said jokingly, "If you don't feed them, they don't make as big a mess."

I thought he was joking, but he wasn't. All of his animals were thin and neglected. But the joke was on him. From that day until the day he was transferred, he had helpers that he knew not of. Benedict left at 4:00 p.m. and I left at 5:00 p.m. Right after he left, the senior keeper and I would slip down and give all of his animals all the food they needed to thrive—and, oh yes, to make a big mess. His new senior keeper also made him keep his corrals clean.

Six months later Benedict was fired for intentionally driving a truck into a telephone pole.

I had occasion worked with his father and noticed he had a propensity to tease animals. He would delight in holding treats just out of the reach of the orangutans and chimps at the health center. He also would give them lit cigarettes and laugh loudy if they burned themselves.

Benedict's father was best known for having been attacked by Sam, the Bactrian camel. Sam knocked him down and grabbed his leg in his mouth. He dashed him up and down and tried to squash his head with his enormous foot. Another keeper risked his own life to save Benedict's father. He had to hit the enraged camel with a shovel and hold him off until the injured man could be dragged from the exhibit. Prior to this, many keepers had reported seeing Benedict's father offering hay to Sam. When Sam would extend his lips to get the hay, Benedict's father would grasp them with his pliers and hold him there until he chose to let him go. He, like his son, had a terrible need to dominate the wild animals. That's how they gained their identity and sense of importance.

It wasn't difficult to calculate the impact of Benedict's father's example. Benedict had learned his irreverence for life from his father.

When the Scripture teaches that the sins of the parent visit the children unto the third and fourth generation (Exodus 20:5), I take it to mean that children keep picking up the values of the parents. Providing a good example is essential to raising decent children.

One Saturday morning I was walking by the black rhino's exhibit and was angered by what I saw. There were two boys on either side of their father throwing some rocks they had collected at the rhinos. They were rather large rocks and the boys were throwing with all their might. The father wasn't saying or doing anything. He was just watching them pelt the rhinos mercilessly. I yelled at the boys to stop and they did.

"Are these your boys?" I asked the father sternly.

"Yeah," he answered defensively.

I looked at him for a moment wondering what to say next, then I asked, "If you didn't want to be responsible for them, why did you have them?"

He didn't know what to say.

"Listen, if you want to help them behave then you can see the rest of the zoo. If not, the front gate is that way. At any rate, I'm going to have security keep an eye on you."

As I walked away, I overheard him say that if they embarrassed him again he would beat them silly.

We saw a lot of cruelty at the zoo. I helped pick up marshmallows concealing razor blades and fish hooks. I asked myself what kind of tortured mind would do that? I participated in several surgeries to repair golden eagles shot by local hunters. What a waste of majestic animal. I remember grabbing a huge chunk of asphalt out of the hands of a twelve-year-old boy who was going to throw it onto an alligator. He screamed, "You can't prove I was going to throw it."

What darkness resides in a man's mind that allows these infringements and much worse? Albert Schweitzer give us some insight in this reflection of his own childhood from his book, *Reverence for Life*:

> While I was still going to the village school we had a dog with a light brown coat, named Phylax. Like many others of his kind, he could not endure a uniform, and always went for the postman. I was, therefore, commissioned to keep him in order whenever the postman came, for he was inclined to bite, and had already been guilty of the crime of attacking a policeman. I therefore used to take a switch and drive him into a corner of the yard, and keep him there till the postman had gone. What a feeling of pride it gave me to stand, like a wild beast tamer, before him while he barked and showed his teeth, and to control him with blows of the switch whenever he tried to break out of the corner! But this feeling of pride did not last. When, later in the day, we sat side by side as friends, I blamed myself for having struck him; I knew that I could keep him back from the postman if I held him by his collar and stroked him. But when the fatal hour came round again I yielded once more to the pleasurable intoxication of being a wild beast tamer!

These kinds of flaws are in all of us to some degree because of the Fall. What happened in Eden broke four relationships: man with God, man with man, man with himself, and man with nature.

For now, we must be commanded to be kind to animals

because it's not something that comes naturally. Proverbs 12:10 shares, "A righteous man has regard for the life of his beast." Jesus tells us that He approves of the idea of helping an animal in trouble even if it means breaking the Sabbath (Luke 13:15, 14:5) He sees the fall of the sparrow (Matthew 10:29). The Lord is acquainted with every bird (Psalm 50:11). Do you know how many birds there are? Billions. And yet God considers all the animals His private property (Psalm 50:10).

Animals cruelty is a terrible sin. How wonderful that the new heaven and the new earth will be free of it.

> The wolf shall dwell with the lamb,
> and the leopard shall lie down with the kid,
> and the calf and the lion and the fatling together,
> and a little child shall lead them.
> The cow and the bear shall feed;
> their young shall lie down together;
> and the lion shall eat straw like the ox.
> And the suckling child shall play
>   on the hole of the asp,
> and the weaned child shall put his hand
>   on the adder's den.
>   Isaiah 11:6–8

Isn't this great? You don't want to miss it. So be sure to be there.

Birds and Bees

Four million, four hundred thousand different species of animals—can you imagine? That is the number of animals God spoke into existence during the fifth and sixth days of creation. That breaks down to 2,200,000 per day or roughly 91,667 species per hour, 1,528 species per minute, or 25.5 new species per second. Now, add to this the amazing fact, that with a few exceptions, He was creating males and females. It means that God was cranking out 51 different anatomies per second, each with its own behavior, unique appearance, and ecological purpose. Every species has been assigned specific and appropriate behaviors for both its sexes. Let me illustrate.

The female black widow spider is four times as large as the male, who is not black at all but white and gold. She is a deadly huntress and knows every inch of her web by feel. She is also blind. When the male comes to court her, he plucks the web at a constant rhythm which calms the throbbing black temptress. Then she quietly awaits his approach. Every few steps he plucks again so that she will not respond as if he were just any insect in her web. He strokes her with his delicate front leg and begins the mating process. He is exhausted after mating and in a weakened condition usually stumbles as he attempts to leave the web. The irregular vibrations trigger her instincts to kill and he is quickly overtaken. Without emotion she adds him to her macabre pantry of stored delicacies.

Sea lion males are a study in rage and passion during breeding season. The males hit the rocky beaches and establish territories for the harems they will build when the females arrive. They fight constantly and brutally, not even taking time to eat. By the time the females arrive, the younger or weaker males have been driven off and the main bulls begin to claim and fight for as many females as they can get. The females have been pregnant for three hundred and fifty days, and they begin to give birth almost as soon as they arrive. Shortly thereafter, the males initiate a brief courtship and mating period. Then they lose interest and no longer dote over their females. Keeping their territory becomes their consuming passion. They will defend it viciously, crashing across rocks and the beach, at times crushing their mates and young to attack an invading male.

Elephants are a matriarchal society. The females call the shots. When the male elephants reach adolescence, they are driven from the main herds to form small groups of males, or they become solitary. They are only tolerated during the breeding season and then driven away again when breeding is completed.

The pied hornbill (an exotic bird with an enormous beak) finds a tree with a hollow apartment. He drives the female into it, then seals her inside with mud. She is not allowed to leave this confinement until the young are ready to leave the nest. Everything the family needs is shoved through the small opening he has left for that reason.

The rattlesnake breeding ritual is a brief erotic study. When he discovers a female during mating season, the male rise above her to full stature and sways back and forth in a captivating ballet. She responds in kind, then they entwine. After mating, he crawls away (that snake in the grass!) never to see her again. She carries the young and gives birth to live babies, which are on their own from their first day in the world.

Penguins mate for life, although they spend more than half of every year separated. The Adele penguins have a ceremony. They present a rock to their beloved. If she accepts it, the pair bond is sealed and they are mated for life. It's "with this rock, I thee wed."

Wolves also mate for life. They live most of the year in small family units, forming packs only in deep winter when it is to their advantage. Because mice are hibernating and therefore unavailable as a food source, the wolves must bring down hooved animals to survive. The males love their mates and provide 50 percent of the sacrificial care of the young. They are the ideal family model.

When we come to man, we cannot discern a consistent method of male and female behavior. You see, in many relationships the male is consumed by the female's dominance and fares no better than the male black widow.

Many males consumed by their careers spend all their time building their territory. They crush their children and pursue extramarital affairs. They act like sea lions.

Some females drive off their males with unattractive fury and make it difficult for the fathers to visit children, just like the elephants do.

Some men force their women to stay home and keep them subjected, like hornbills.

Then there are those who form a partnership. They are helpmates. They work together to raise the young in a cooperative venture, like wolves. Some mate for life, like the penguins.

One of two things is true: Either man is the only species out of four million, four hundred thousand without an assigned method of relating male and female or we have an assigned method that we are not following. What do you think?

God's Word gives us a good picture of what He had in mind in Ephesians 5:21–33.

Verse 21:
Husbands and wives are to show honor to each other.

Verses 22–24:
Wives, make your husband feel like he's important. Respect him. Treat him like he's someone special, somebody worthwhile.

Verses 25–33:
Husbands, love your wives in a sacrificial way. Serve her needs in such a way that you set her apart from all others as unique and special. Encourage her to be everything she can be. Nourish her and cherish her. Then you'll become totally united.

We don't see this kind of marriage very often. Do you think we've become too focused on who is going to meet our personal needs? Do you think we live in a selfish age?

For understanding this, that in the last days there will come times of stress. For men will be lovers of self...
2 Timothy 3:1–2

Protect Us From Those Who Protect Us

Cowboys and Indians, cats and dogs, Russians and Americans, security guards and animal keepers—they are all sets of classical enemies. I suppose this statement needs an explanation.

Security guards and animal keepers have a built-in basis for misunderstanding. It begins with the way they dress. Security guards wear neatly-pressed uniforms, ties, and their shoes are so shiny that you may catch a glimpse of your own reflection as they pass by. Their fingernails look manicured and their hands are soft and smooth; no calluses need apply, thank you. By quitting time they are still neatly pressed and should they walk by, you may pick up the delicate remembrance of their shaving lotion as it echoes their departure. What can I say? They are eight-by-ten glossies.

Animal keepers dress in work clothes: dark brown pants and tan shirts. They perform hard physical labor and they sweat profusely. By morning break they may smell like twenty minutes of brisk basketball. Their shoes never shine and shouldn't even be discussed in mixed company. Their hands are weathered and calloused and could be used to plane a door. They are of the earth.

Security deals with the public. They know little of the animals and they are proud of it. They couldn't tell you the difference between a wallaby and a wombat.

Keepers talk animals, breathe animals, and dream animals. Do you want to know where animal keepers go on their vacations? To other zoos. That should tell you something.

The fact that security knows little about animals is not the rub. No indeed. The real problem is that keepers never see security guards do anything that remotely resembles work. They see them walk by, but zoo patrons do that. They see them drive by, and that's even worse because that's accomplished in a sitting position. As far as the keepers can observe, security just walks back and forth, drives back and forth, takes coffee breaks, and gets paid for it.

In all fairness, we had a fine security staff at the zoo, and still do. But there were some guards who seemed to reinforce all the suspicions and accusations that the keepers made about them. Let me illustrate.

In 1969 our Australian dingo dogs had puppies—five yellow balls of mischief that charmed every passerby. The keeper that cared for them played with them every chance he got, and they became very tame. They knew no strangers and spent a good deal of their day at the front of their cage licking people's fingers and accepting as much affection as they could solicit. Now if you know wild animals, a dingo dog is a very distinctive breed. But if you don't, it's just another old yeller dog. It looks like a cross between a German shepherd and a yellow Labrador retriever. You might find something similar any day you visited your local animal shelter.

The zoo was a popular hangout for hippies in the late sixties. One of them formed an affection with the dingo pups and conceived a plan. It was a simple plan. Smuggle wire cutters under your trench coat and cut just enough wire so that you might liberate one puppy. If you came on a weekday, no one would ever notice what you had done. That's just what he did. He and his girlfriend paid their admission and walked straight to our Australian section. I'm confident that she stood watch while he labored to snip the wire in six places. He bent up the wire and—presto!—he possessed his own dingo pup.

Oh, but he wasn't out of the woods yet. He was two-fifths of a mile from the front gate. He had picked the most wiggly puppy of the five. It was noisy, too. They began to walk to the front gate when they were stopped. Can't you image how their hearts began to pound?

The security guard spoke with practiced authority, "Hey! What you got under that coat? You want to show it to me?" The hippie looked paralyzed. He opened up his coat and extended the wiggly puppy toward the security guard who patted it on the head and said, "I didn't want to hold your puppy, I just wanted to see it. Didn't you folks see the 'No Pets' sign at the front gate? We don't allow pets because they might give our animals a new disease or something. I'm afraid that I'm going to have to escort you to the front gate and make sure that you get the pup off the premises."

That's just what that security guard did. He gave them the equivalent of a police escort right to the front gate while the hippie and his girlfriend apologized all the way to their car. They apologized so much that the security guard began to apologize for the size of the small "no pets allowed" sign.

Boy, did the keepers have fun with that story. They said that it was a good thing the hippie didn't try to steal an elephant or the security guard might have gotten a hernia helping him carry it out.

Not too long after that, a night security guard offered the coup degrâce to any hopes of a reconciliation. A gentle female chimpanzee escaped from her cage at the old zoo two miles away, where the chimps were being held until their quarters at the health center became available once again. It was three in the morning, and the security guard caught a glimpse of the ambling ape in the high beams of his security vehicle. He radioed the security center at the main zoo for instructions as to what he should do. The security center phoned Dr. Cooper at home and advised him of the emergency. They asked him what the guard should do. Not knowing that it was one of the very gentle females, Dr. Cooper advised the security officer on the scene to do anything necessary to keep the chimp from leaving the area. It could be a very dangerous animal roaming the neighborhoods surrounding Griffith Park. As Dr. Cooper was hanging up the phone, he thought that it may have been better if he had not made the chimp seem so dangerous. He recalled that the particular security guard on the scene was a gun enthusiast. Dr. Cooper arrived at the old zoo ten minutes too late. The sweet young female was already dead. She had been shot to death by the night security guard.

The officer's story was that he had stepped out of his vehicle to follow the chimp and she charged him. The examination revealed that the chimp had been shot in the back. Although Dr. Cooper tried his best to explain that he had set the security guard up to be terrified, the keepers just wouldn't buy it. They hounded that man until the day he quit the zoo!

I have many times since tried to put myself in the place of that security guard. The zoo is an eerie place at night and surpasses a graveyard for down-right frightfulness. I don't believe in ghosts, but I do believe in animals. The years have proven that animals do get out, and you could never be sure that you were not sharing a path with an escaped lion or a bear. The security guard couldn't have known which chimps were dangerous and which ones were not. Nobody could have known in the dark. I'm not sure what I would have done if a chimp approached me on a dark night at the old zoo. Well, it was a long while before the hard feelings were abated.

About the time they had, something else happened. It was five-thirty in the evening on a Thursday and the red phone began to ring at the security office. It was an ominous signal. It meant that one of the keepers at the reptile house had been bitten by a deadly snake. The system is arranged so that as soon as the keeper is bitten, he could walk to a red phone and simply take it off the hook. This would cause the red phone to ring in the security office and trigger a whole sequence of events to unfold. Supervisors would be notified, County General would be called, and a security guard would rush to the reptile house to assist with emergency transportation.

Everything went like clockwork except for the part where the security guard rushes to the reptile house to provide transportation. He rushed to the reptile house, all right, and he range the doorbell. Nobody answered, so he range again and again. It wouldn't be difficult to deduce that the man inside was probably unconscious by now and couldn't answer the door. So thought the security guard. He walked around the outside of the building yelling, "Is anybody hurt in there?" And of course he received no reply. One of the senior animal keepers leaving a bit late for home overheard the yelling and ran to investigate.

"What's wrong?" asked the out-of-breath senior keeper.

"The red phone's been pulled. It's ringing like crazy down at the security center."

"What are you doing out here then, you dumb -----------?" he yelled. The senior keeper rushed inside the building and searched the maze of interconnected rooms that made up the reptile house. Nobody was there. It was later discovered that a water pipe had burst and shorted out the red phone line.

When the senior keeper came out of the building he was blazing mad. "What's your problem, son?" he asked.

"I'm afraid of snakes, okay?" replied the embarrassed guard.

"Son, this is a heck of a time to admit it. A man could have lost his life because of you, you know."

The question was posed after that incident, "If security's job is to protect us from the people, who's going to protect us from security?"

Even so, my mind was to be changed forever as to security's worth. I'm deathly allergic to the sting of honeybees, and one sparkling morning I was stung on the arm. I staggered to the chief keeper's office and announced my dilemma. He was familiar with the gravity of my situation and notified security. With all that had gone on before, I had reservations about putting my life in security's hands. I was amazed when they arrived at the chief's office in less than forty-five seconds, and in no time we were speeding along the freeway to a hospital in nearby Glendale. From the sting to the treatment, less than eight minutes had passed. They were kind to me, and after the incident I was asked several times how I was doing by the security guards who had helped me out. I felt just like the man who had been robbed in the Good Samaritan story. It changed my whole perspective of the security guards when they helped me in that crisis.

As I began to talk with the security staff, I found out they were really a super group of guys. Their job was with people and mine was with animals. I can tell you right now I wouldn't have traded jobs with those guys if I were paid twice my salary.

Have you read the parable of the Good Samaritan lately? You can find it in Luke 10:25–37. Read it. Then ask yourself if you have been building up a prejudice. Chances are that the Lord is calling you to love the person who has come to mind.

I have found C.S. Lewis' Mere Christianity to be a most helpful book. It makes me think more than any other book that I have ever read. In the chapter entitled "Charity" resides a most provocative paragraph:

> I pointed out in the chapter on Forgiveness that our love for ourselves does not mean that we like ourselves. It means that we wish our own good. In the same way Christian Love (or charity) for our neighbors is quite a different thing from liking or affection. We "like" or are "fond of" some people, and not of others. It is important to understand that this natural "liking" is neither a sin nor a virtue, anymore than your likes and dislikes of food are a sin or a virtue. It is just a fact. But of course, what we do about it is either sinful or virtuous.

What we should do when we find that we are not liking someone is to perform an act of kindness toward him. It is easier to love someone you are helping than someone you are hurting.

Just A Walk In The Park

The zoo security guard pulled his light green Plymouth Valiant to an abrupt halt as he approached the aquatics section. There in the lengthening shadows of early evening was a large male chimpanzee walking slowly toward the back of the California sea lion exhibit. The guard had been at the zoo long enough to recognize that this was Toto. The zoo had eight chimpanzees in the collection. Of the eight, Toto was the worst possible chimp to be three-quarters of a mile from his cage. He was a former circus chimp, and in all likelihood he had been badly abused. By human standards, Toto was crazy, psychotic, totally unpredictable. He could be gentle and friendly one moment and frenzied and violent the next.

The security guard rolled up his window and locked all the car doors. He reached for his walkie-talkie. He clicked it to the "on" position and it crackled to life. With his eyes fixed on the chimp that was now walking slowly toward his vehicle, he pressed the "send" button and whispered, "Sam, this is Joey...you there?"

He lifted the button and heard Sam reply, "Yeah, I'm here. What's up? Sounds like you're looking at a ghost...over?"

"I wish I were. I'm in back of the chief keeper's shack just below the California sea lion exhibit, looking at Toto...over."

"Sounds like we have a problem. I'll notify the acting director and the capture team. Do your best to keep track of his whereabouts. Keep me posted. And Joey, be real careful. From what I've heard, Toto is bad news."

Joey kept track of Toto, and for whatever reason, Toto stayed near the chief's shack. He was, for all intents and purposes, lost. His zoo cage had been his territory for two years, and without help he would not be able to find his way back to it. Not knowing where he was, Toto was left with the problem of having nowhere to run. In his tangled mind he imagined he could be in enemy-occupied territory and was on the verge of emotional frenzy. He probably stayed in the area to be near the security guard who was keeping an eye on him.

Most of the capture team arrived at the same time and wisely stayed in their cars, waiting for Dr. Gale, the assistant director. Dr. Gale was an excellent animal-capture man worth waiting for, and the truth was that he would not have tolerated it any other way.

Toto was preoccupied with the sounds and smells of the immediate area and was satisfied that his company was staying in their cars. When Dr. Gale arrived, it was very dark and only the horizon gave a hint that the sun had just set for the night. The zoo's dark green shrubbery nearly absorbed Toto's silhouette and only his occasional movement betrayed his whereabouts. Dr. Gale directed the security guard to watch Toto, then motioned for the capture team to follow him out of the area. Once out of Toto's sight, they got out of their cars and listened to Dr. Gale's plan.

"We can't dart Toto with the capture gun; it is too dark to know if we hit him. He might fall into a pool, or worst of all, we may miss and scare him so that he leaves the zoo. Then he'd need to be shot before he hurt someone in the local neighborhood. If any of you have change, give it to me." They looked at each other, wondering what Dr. Gale had up his sleeve. But they knew him well enough not to question him. The change added up to a little less than two dollars. Dr. Gale sighed as he held it in his hand. He gave Bob Spelling fifty cents of it and told him to run and get a Coke from the nearest vending machine. He told the other men to drive up to the zoo's health center, open all the doors, turn on all the lights and wait there for him and Toto. He told them he was going to attempt to walk Toto back to his cage; but he felt the fewer animal-care staff that Toto saw, the less chance there would be of Toto's flipping out and becoming violent.

Bob Spelling returned with the Coke and handed it to Dr. Gale who took a sip, and smiled a "wish-me-luck" smile. He waited for the men to clear the area, then walked slowly toward Toto. When he was nearing the escaped chimp he could see that Toto was a bit apprehensive, and even in the dark he could see that Toto was beginning to stand; his hair was on end, and he looked as if he were about to charge.

Dr. Gale spoke softly, "You want something to drink, Toto?" Toto settled down and walked slowly forward and looked briefly at the cup and then into Dr. Gale's eyes. He reached for the man's hand and pulled it and the cup to his mouth and moaned contentedly. He poured most of the cup into his mouth. Dr. Gale was wishing the zoo served larger Cokes, because his plan was to lure him from vending machine to vending machine until they reached Toto's cage. But if Toto were going to finish everything so quickly, he might not follow to the next reward. Even worse, he might want more, and there would be no more to give him. It never took much to disturb Toto, and that was the last thing Dr. Gale wanted to happen alone in the dark in the middle of the zoo. He was already questioning the wisdom of his own plan and looked around to see if any of the men were still nearby to suggest

Plan B. But he was alone. He wasn't really alone; there was a psychotic former circus chimp standing at his side drinking the last drop of Coke out of a cup that seemed smaller than ever.

Dr. Gale saw the chief keeper's building and concluded that he might buy some time if he could lock Toto in the building. So he offered Toto his hand, and Toto took it—something he would have done as a young chimp but may not do for long as an old chimp who was six times as strong as the man who as leading him. Dr. Gale removed the keys from his pocket and unlocked the chief keeper's office. He walked into the dark office, hoping Toto would follow. He did. It was darker inside than out and Dr. Gale waited until he was sure Toto was fully inside.

Then Dr. Gale made a quick move and slipped out the door as quickly as he could. He slammed the door and locked it. His heart was pounding and beads or perspiration were forming on his forehead. He wiped it with his handkerchief and walked on his tiptoes to see if Toto was calm inside. He shaded his eyes from the glare of the street light that created reflections on the window and stared into the darkness of the office. He strained his eyes to see Toto, but could not locate the chimp. He felt a hand on his shoulder and slowly turned to find himself face-to-face with a disturbed Toto. In a mimicking fashion, Toto was also shielding his eyes from the reflection as he, too, stared into the darkness, trying to discover what had frightened the doctor out of the office.

"Let's go home, Toto," said the doctor, resigned to the first plan. Toto followed him to the next vending machine where he purchased a small box of Good and Plenty candies. Toto enjoyed them immensely, but would stop, sit down, and suck on them. So progress was somewhat impeded. Dr. Gale was limited to one more purchase, and he was not even halfway to the health center. The wizened vet noticed a drinking fountain and turned the handle to show Toto that he could get a drink. Toto drank copious drafts of water and was captured by the novelty of the drinking device.

A lion roared from its night quarters. Toto stood straight up and rocked back and forth as if he were going to begin an aggressive display. He ran toward the lion and screamed one loud scream as a warning to his unseen enemy. Then he looked back at Dr. Gale as if to say, "Well, I guess that takes care of that." Dr. Gale praised him in a soft voice and rewarded him with a Good and Plenty.

The Good and Plentys ran out, so he made one last purchase. A Payday candy bar slid out of the vending machine. Toto watched with interest as its wrapper was peeled away and a small piece was handed to him. Dr. Gale walked faster now, knowing he was on borrowed time. Toto grunted a "wait for me" sound and ran on all fours to catch up. The Payday was clearly a favorite choice. The chimp tugged at his benefactor's pant leg for another piece. Progress was now at a sufficient pace, and it looked as though they might make it to the health center after all.

As they rounded the corner at the mountain zebra exhibit, a terror-filled event took place. Ed Alonzo, the principal keeper, was waiting fifty yards away under a street light, monitoring the doctor's journey. If Dr. Gale got in trouble, Ed wanted to be there to help. But now Ed was in trouble. When Toto saw Ed under the street light, he stood up and hooted. He bolted away from Dr. Gale and ran at full speed toward the frozen principal keeper. Toto had injured others. Two keepers at the zoo had only nine fingers because of Toto. Ed fully expected to be bitten and beaten within an inch of his life, so he braced himself for the attack.

Toto looked menacing as he charged closer and closer. Ed swallowed and prepared himself for the awesome impact he was about to experience. At the last possible second, Toto pulled up short and stood up in front of Ed to greet him. Ed had been his keeper a few years before and Toto was merely saying hello with a great deal of enthusiasm. Seeing a person that Toto remembered fondly had thoroughly piqued his interest. He had grown tired of the night's adventure, and Ed probably represented care and security. Toto reached for Ed's hand, which was shaking noticeably from the massive dose of adrenalin which had just been released into his system. The baton had been handed to Ed, so the last one hundred yards were his to accomplish.

He and Toto walked up a narrow overgrown path, and when they reached the top, they could see the health center in full view. Toto released Ed's hand and again ran full speed until he had entered the health center's surgery door. He walked down the well-lighted hallway into the cage room and stood peering through the open door of his cage as if he were trying to make up his mind, "Shall I go in, or shall I stay out?" It was at this point that Bill Dickman, a brave and foolish keeper, ran full swing into Toto, bumping him into his cage and slamming the door behind him. Toto hooted his displeasure, but he decided to be forgiving because he was so glad to be home.

This story reminds me that Jesus was willing to leave the safety of heaven to help me find my way back to Him. He cared about you and me so much that no risk was too great to ensure that we could come home. There was one difference in His story, however. He died to make it possible. This story also illustrates three great truths of life: (1) We will need to help others find the way to Jesus. (2) We will need to help Christians who have lost their way to find their way home. We are our brother's keeper. And (3), be sure to make friends who will come and get you when you get lost.

Good For A Laugh

I love a good laugh. It is one of God's greatest inventions. Psalm 2:4 begins, "He who sits in the heavens laughs." The following stories are offered for your enjoyment. I hope they cause you to laugh, especially if you need to laugh.

Jambie

About a year before I began my career with the zoo, a legend died. His name was Jambie. He was a large adult male orangutan. I never met the fellow, but his delightful episodes were told and retold, as all great tales should be. You see, Jambie was an incurable practical joker. His specialty was water jokes.

Over the years, Jambie learned the art of trading. He would throw food that he didn't care for out of the cage in hopes that someone would give him something he really liked. What happened most of the time was that a person would retrieve the castaway food and throw it back to Jambie. Jambie was a bit frustrated that no trade was effected, so at some point he conceived a plan to humiliate the naïve zoo patrons who were missing the point.

Now it may be helpful for you to know that Jambie could hold nearly a gallon of water in his cavernous mouth. To entice the inept traders, he learned to drop his trading item close to the wire of his cage. When the patron would bend over the guardrail to fetch the food, Jambie would climb quickly to a position above them and spew nearly a gallon of liquid all over his or her back.

He learned the art of positioning for other purposes also. He would grind up his monkey biscuits and sprinkle them just outside his cage...but within the reach of his monstrous hand. From the base of his palm to the tip of his fingers it measured nineteen inches. He would lay his hand down near the crumbs and wait with patience for the peacock's hen and her chicks to come close to the bait. With a sudden sweep of his hand he had new and animated toys. He would bring them into his cage and play with them for hours.

The Weekend Authority

I have listened to hundreds of zoo patrons say some incredible things about the animals, but none more incredible than what Henry told Mildred about the beisa oryx. A beisa oryx is an African antelope. It is one of the larger members of the family, standing about three and one-half feet at the shoulder. Its slender horns curve gracefully another two feet above the head. It is a combination of subtle gray, brown, black and white—a strikingly beautiful animal.

Henry studied the oryx for several seconds. You could tell he was impressed. By the look of his clothing and the sound of his accent, my guess was that he was visiting from the Ozarks of Arkansas. I couldn't be sure, but certainly he was from somewhere in the Deep South. His voice caught my attention. I was inside a barn talking to an animal keeper about a medication he would be giving one of the animals on his string when Henry began to lecture his family on what he had learned by reading the zoo sign.

I peeked out the door and saw Henry surrounded by his three little boys. They were all dressed in overalls and wore no shirts. Mildred, his wife, stood where I would have stood if my family were dressed that way in Southern California—about twenty feet away. It didn't do any good, though, because he kept shouting some new particle of information he had gleaned from a sign.

"Hey, Mildred," he hollered, "you won't believe this! This here oryx as a gestation period of 267 days. That is a mighty long time to digest your food."

"What does it mean, Daddy?" ventured one of his cherubs.

"Billy Joe, it means that what this animal eats today won't be eliminated until next February." Then he sighed and said, "Ain't that amazing?"

It was mid-July.

Now You See it...Now You Don't...Now You Do!

It was clearly entered into the daily log: "Six puppies born to Mr. and Mrs. Coyote." Everybody thought they were cute. But Charlie, their keeper, found them irresistible. As soon as their mother began to take periodic rests from the coyote puppies, Charlie would slip in to tame them. They responded quickly to his affection.

One little female was a standout. She was gentle, affectionate, and would stay with Charlie longer than all the rest. Charlie became very attached to her and was soon locking all the others out with mom so that he could play with his little beloved. Before long, he decided that this pup was far too special to grow up in a zoo. He made the decision to take her home and slipped her out in his lunch pail.

Not too many days passed before the senior keeper noticed that there were five puppies rather than six. He approached

Charlie to see if he knew what might have happened to the missing puppy. Charlie told Al that he never remembered there being six. Al must have counted one twice. Al was nobody's fool, but he decided to buy the story for a couple of reasons. First, the coyotes had no real value; and second, their future in the zoo world was very uncertain. If Charlie had swiped it, it was sure to be loved and well-cared for.

Charlie lived in an apartment building with his wife, Cindy. She fell in love with the pup as soon as she saw it agreed they should keep it. They had a sterling relationship with their landlady and she reluctantly gave them permission to care for it. They convinced her that it was simply a mongrel dog, but as the puppy grew their landlady grew skeptical. She would periodically ask, "That isn't a wolf, is it?"

"No, it's just a terrier-shepherd mix," said Charlie and Cindy.

Well, the landlady became more and more focused on determining the puppy's origin. Charlie and Cindy could see the growing concern on her face, and they knew in their hearts that they were going to have to give back the puppy or surely face the chance of getting caught for stealing. They had no friends who wanted a coyote, so Charlie decided he would return her to the zoo. He drove his car directly to her exhibit and returned the coyote pup to the cage. It was very early, and no one witnessed the glad reunion. Although she had been away nearly six months, she was well-received by her family and readjusted to zoo life quite nicely.

It wasn't until Charlie's day off that anything out of the ordinary was noted. His relief keeper came to Al, the senior keeper, and said, "You have to come and see this, Al. I can't believe it."

Al followed the relief keeper to the coyote exhibit and stepped inside the cage. He was immediately approached by a tame, teenaged coyote that licked his hands and whined for attention.

"I've never seen anything like this in my life," said the dumbfounded keeper.

"Neither have I," replied Al, as he stroked his chin thoughtfully.

Al never pursued the subject with Charlie, so far as I know, but he did mention to Charlie that he'd better take a course in basic math so he could keep an accurate count of his string. Keepers speculated for months about how a coyote became tame overnight.

Give 'Em an Eyeful

Snakes have never terrified me, but the guys who worked in the reptile house were frightening. A number of us enjoyed a good practical joke, but the reptile keepers carried theirs to the very brink of impracticality.

I will not here betray all their secrets. But if by some quirk of fate the reader should someday be exposed to the possibility of being caught in their favorite ploy, I must, in good conscience, prepare them.

First, let me tell you that the guys who work reptiles are very intelligent, a breed of their own. They know their business and must maintain absolute concentration lest they make a mistake. In their arena, their first mistake could be their last. Many of the snakes are so deadly that their bites could not be survived. Unlike the rest of the keepers, the reptile keepers spent their days entirely indoors. There are no windows through which to view the sky. And walking through the seemingly endless corridors of the facility, one could easily lose track of where he is. There are many aquariums that rest on inside shelves which are never seen by the majority of the public. They hold a variety of poisonous and nonpoisonous snakes, and some folks are forever wondering if anything has recently escaped. The color scheme, if there is a scheme, is devoid of charm. And the atmosphere is sterile, institutional, and scientific.

The reptile keepers had a great sting operation, and their favorite marks in the early days were new keepers. If you were a new keeper and they were offered the opportunity to take you on a tour, they would jump at the chance. They would begin at one end of the building, which must be about fifty yards long, and dazzle you with facts and statistics. You simply could not resist the urge to admire them for their absolute command of their subject, reptiles. You would be introduced to the world of rattlesnakes and exotic frogs and toads. You might get to hold a variety of nonpoisonous snakes, like king snakes or gopher snakes, and let me tell you, you would find yourself trusting them—the keepers, not the snakes, Well, both actually. The point was, they had you just where they wanted you by the time you three-quarters of the way through. You would do just about anything they told you to do, because you knew that what they were telling you to do was okay. It was safe.

About this time you would come to a cage. Hanging from the back of the cage was a pair of goggles, the type you would wear if you were using a table saw. They were next to a sign that immediately caught your interest. It read, "Beware of Spitting Cobra!" You would be guided skillfully into the wonderful world of cobras and their behaviors and myths. You would find yourself asking questions about he effects of the venom on your eyes and skin. You would discover that blindness may occur, along with unbelievable pain. Then in a very matter-of-fact, nothing-to-worry-about way you would be invited to look into the spitting cobra's cage. It meant moving closer and leaning forward a little bit so that you could look over the top of the terrarium. If you hesitated, they would nonchalantly say, "No problem," or "Nothing to worry about," and then you would trust them again. While you were gazing through the screen trying to focus on the snake at the bottom of the cage, they would squeeze a rubber bulb with warm water in it. It would course through a system of tubes and gush into your eyes while they yelled, "Look out!"

There were a lot of adults who lost most of their dignity in those moments, as they said and did things we are usually spared in public life.

The laughter that echoed through that hallway bordered on the demonic, and I believe that there are many who take comfort in the fact that these men will someday stand before God on Judgment Day. They won't be holding any rubber bulbs in their hands then. No sir-ee.

Where Trouble Follows

A zoo is a terrifying place to work for the accident prone. Bill Whitecross was. In the seven years that I worked at the Los Angeles Zoo, I cannot recall seeing Bill without a bandage, cast, crutch, or some other evidence that he had been on the losing end of an untimely skirmish. Docile animals that normally adored people hurt Bill Whitecross. In fact, there was a rumor that has persisted to this day that even mealworms attacked Bill Whitecross. Now I never saw that happen, but I saw enough to convince myself that his presence should be shunned during lightning storms.

A group of us were at the white rhino barn one afternoon—for what reason I cannot remember. Sonny and Cher, our white rhinos, were pressing at the gate, hoping that someone would scratch behind their ears or around their eyes. They were very tame and could be ridden if we didn't mind arriving at their chosen destination. Rhinos go where they want to go…and who's to stop them?

Bill decided to step just inside the gate to accommodate the passive giants. It turned out to be one more opportunity for lightning to strike. Sonny went into instant ecstasy as Bill aggressively scratched behind his ear. Sonny closed his kindly eye and stepped forward to get even closer to the human that was showing him the kindness. Unfortunately, he stepped and stayed on Bill's foot. Now a white rhino weighs about seven thousand pounds, so Bill was experiencing the same sensation you might experience if you set a Volkswagen on your foot. He tried not to look foolish as he oooed and ahhhed, but he did not succeed. Several of us tried to push Sonny away gently, but he did not want to go, so he didn't. He just stood there on Bill's foot, waiting for more affection. Bill, however, was somewhat distracted.

The rhino finally and mercifully stepped forward. Bill moaned with relief. He removed his shoe and all agreed that Bill would never need swim fins again.

Bill spent a good deal of his zoo career at the reptile house, serving as its senior keeper. Senior keepers have much less work to keep them busy than do keepers, and in Bill's case that turned against him. Looking for amusement nearly cost him his life.

Down at the very west end of the reptile house was an African python named Jeanie. Jeanie was another one of our tame animals. Bill decided that he would feed Jeanie a dead rat by hand. This had been attempted successfully on several other occasions, but never by Bill. Bill waited until a group of zoo patrons was in front of her massive cage. Then he dangled the tempting morsel in front of her emotionless eyes. He must have had a fleeting glimpse that her eyes were clouded over because she was going to shed. He may have had just enough time to think that this may not have been the best time to feed her because she couldn't see the rat clearly. Jeanie, by the way, was fourteen feet long and about twenty inches around. Well, Jeanie was never one to turn down an hors d'oeuvre, and she launched forth. She missed the rat by five inches, but—you guessed it—she grabbed Bill. Her nostrils were aglow with the smell of a rat, and from her perspective, she had grabbed a giant one. She yanked Bill into the cage and quickly threw two coils around the surprised senior keeper. His efforts to extricate himself were absolutely futile, and the terrified zoo patrons sensed they were watching a life-and-death drama. Bill was too embarrassed to call for help and continued to struggle with the adamant python. One of the patrons ran around the building beating on doors until an angry keeper near the other end of the building came out to investigate. The hysterical patron finally conveyed the emergency and three men ran to the aid of their supervisor. He was freed from the coils of the python, but he was never able to escape the retelling of this story.

Cockatoo, Cockatoo

If you ever visit the zoo's Australian section, be sure to stop by the cockatoo exhibit for a while. They are beautiful, entertaining, and some of them even talk. They have often been people's pets before coming to the zoo, and about half of their owners named them Cookie. This is easy to determine because most of the previously owned birds say, "Hello, Cookie."

Mark Gentry enjoyed the ability of being able to impersonate the cockatoos' voices. One could not tell which was the bird and which was Mark. Mark was their keeper. He would often hear patrons attempting to strike up conversations with the cockatoos that talked, and one afternoon he had a bright idea. He stationed himself in the shrubbery next to the exhibit and waiting for some enthusiastic visitors to respond to the cockatoos' endless chatter. If a patron repeated one of the bird's phrases, Mark was set up for several minutes of a Candid Camera-type encounter without a camera.

"Hello, Cookie," offered a bird.

"Hello, Cookie," answered a patron.

"What's your name?" entered Mark, but you couldn't tell it was Mark because he sounded just like the cockatoos.

"My name is Barbara," answered a rather attractive patron. Then she added, "What's yours?"

"Cookie, silly. You just said 'Hello, Cooke,' so I thought you knew," said Mark. Barbara still thought she was talking to a bird. She caught on when one of the birds said, "So, Barbara, what's your telephone number?"

One day a rather loud, critical, overfed, and unattractive lady brought her little tiny husband to the zoo. Perhaps you might form an accurate mental picture if I simply told you that on that day we could account for the whereabouts of at least one of Cinderella's stepsisters. Her face was adorned with a permanent frown and her demeanor suggested that she was just daring something good to happen so she could step on it. Her husband just stood there, "Yes, darling"-ed her as she berated the zoo, its animals, the zoo food, and him.

Mark was in the bushes and one of the cockatoos said, "Hello, Cookie."

The lady stared at the bird for a second and responded with "Hello, Cookie, yourself."

In the twinkling of an eye, Mark responded with, "Hi ya, Fatso."

She gave the closest cockatoo a stare that would have frozen the Medusa, then she clobbered her husband with her purse and said, "Henry, let's get out of here." She stormed off fully convinced that she had been insulted by a bird.

Life truly is a zoo.

About The Author

Gary Richmond has spent most of the last forty years in some type of ministry position and has, at the same time, fostered a life-long love of animals and nature. He spent several years working at the Los Angeles Zoo and was nicknamed "Father Nature" at Forest Home Christian Conference Center because of his expertise in things relating to the natural world. He has authored many books, including *Successful Single Parenting* and a series of childrens' books based on his zoo stories. For the past two decades, Gary has been the pastor to single parents at First Evangelical Free Church in Fullerton, California. He lives in Southern California with his wife, Carol, and near his three children and five grandchildren.

COMING SUMMER 2005

Gary Richmond's Zoo Stories come to life in a brand-new way:
In Your Own Living Room!

A New View From The Zoo Live!

Gary tells some of his favorite Zoo Stories to a live audience and
you are there to experience it: stories leap from the pages
and take on a whole new life in the hands of
this master storyteller.

For Up-To-Date Info, please visit:
www.newviewfromthezoo.com

GIVE A New VIEW
TO SOMEONE SPECIAL

Gary Richmond's wonderful collection
of stories, *A New View From The Zoo*,
makes the perfect gift for almost any
occasion: a birthday, a graduation,
Christmas, or a great way to say "Get
Well Soon."

Share the joy contained within these
pages with a special person today.

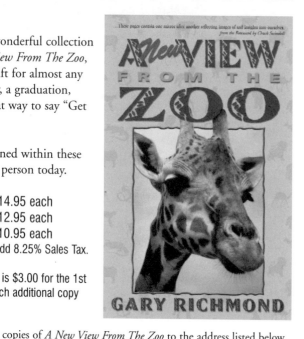

1–5 Copies	$14.95 each
6–15 Copies	$12.95 each
16–more	$10.95 each

California residents add 8.25% Sales Tax.

Shipping & Handling is $3.00 for the 1st
Copy, $1.00 for each additional copy

❑ Please send _____ copies of *A New View From The Zoo* to the address listed below.
I am including Shipping & Handling Charges in accordance with the above
schedule and 8.25% Sales Tax if I am a California resident.

Name: _____

Address: _____

City: _____ State: _____ Zip: _____

Phone Number: _____

E-mail Address: _____

Mail This Form along with a Check or Money Order to:

DMJ Media Group
P.O. Box 1297
La Mirada, CA 90637-1297

Please make checks or money orders payable to "DMJ Media Group"
If you have any questions, please e-mail: sales@dmjmedia.com
or contact us via regular mail at the above address.